Ministers and Martyrs

Mike Aquilina

Ministers and Martyrs

The Ultimate Catholic Guide to the Apostolic Age

SOPHIA INSTITUTE PRESS
Manchester, New Hampshire

Sophia Institute Press
Box 5284, Manchester, NH 03108
1-800-888-9344

www.SophiaInstitute.com

Sophia Institute Press® is a registered trademark of Sophia Institute.

ISBN: 978-1-622822-652

First printing

For Ruth and Glenn Shupp,
Mom and Dad

Contents

Foreword

Jesus did not write books. The Gospels show him reading from the scrolls of the prophets (Luke 4:16–20) but never setting down his own words. *Once* we see him writing—but he was writing in the dust, words that perhaps no one noticed and were soon blown away or erased by footprints.

Jesus did not write books, but he did use words, and he spoke them to his Church—first in the person of his ministers, the Apostles, and then, through his ministers, to the world. What was whispered "in private rooms" as the Apostles awaited the Spirit has been "proclaimed upon the housetops" ever since the first Christian Pentecost.

The Apostles handed on the Faith, and that is the simple meaning of the word *tradition*. It is a "handing on," and it takes place within the Church. The life we know as Catholics today—with its special rites and customs, its Scriptures and its structures—is evident in the records of the apostolic Church. It is there in the small details of the stories we find in the Acts of the Apostles. It is there in the instruction we find in the New Testament letters. The Faith the Apostles practiced and preached in Jerusalem, and took from Jerusalem to the world, is the Faith we practice in our parishes today—and take from our parishes to the world.

Ours is the Faith of the apostolic Church. What was then planted as a seed is now grown and flourishing. Over the years the Church has elaborated on that Faith, but never changed it—has never added anything to it and never taken anything away.

For two thousand years the Church has reflected on the heritage we have received from the Apostles. Popes and councils have developed its doctrine. Artists have depicted its history. Composers have set its gospel to beautiful melodies. We can study the Faith today in catechisms and countless books of theology and apologetics.

Development and elaboration are helpful. But we must not allow ourselves to forget the simple beauty of our salvation—the ordinariness of the setting and the cast of the biblical story. We were saved by a common craftsman from a small, out-of-the-way village. He surrounded himself with people who went unnoticed by the celebrities and power brokers of the day.

The elements of our salvation were likewise common things: the wood of the Cross, wheat bread, simple wine, olive oil, and water.

The events of our salvation took place in a crowded city, as dusty as any other. Jesus carried his Cross through winding streets lined with merchants, pedestrians, gawkers, and vacationers. As his Passion played out, the local law enforcement tried to manage the crowd and keep traffic moving. The Apostles walked those same dusty streets as they began their ministry.

God became flesh and dwelt among us in a particular place, at a particular time, and lived a particular way of life. His Apostles, too, were particular men, chosen not by worldly standards but by divine wisdom.

Our development and elaboration always begin from historical events and facts. History is the foundation, says an old Catholic maxim: *Historia fundamentum est*. And that in itself is an Apostolic impulse. The New Testament tells us that, as Christians, we do "not follow cleverly devised myths" (2 Pet. 1:16). Our Faith is rooted in events that proved to be the pivot of history. We received the Faith we cherish through the testimony of eyewitnesses—the original disciples who gave their lives to Jesus Christ as ministers and martyrs.

It is good for us to go back, often, to study the lives of the early Christians. Their faith had a freshness, a sense of surprise, that we can learn and recover for ourselves. God, after all, is as youthful as ever; Jesus still has the capacity to suddenly astonish people who think they know him well.

The Apostles can seem so far away from us. They lived two thousand years ago, in a time before mass media, electricity, and rapid transit. But they share our human nature, and that is unchanging. They also share our vocation: to spread the gospel in a world that's indifferent or hostile to God. Even the words they use that sometimes seem unusual or technical—words such as *minister, martyr, eucharist, gospel,* and *scripture*—were, in their original context, terms for common things in ordinary life. We use their functional equivalents every day and rarely (if ever) make the connection.

This book—by my friend and sometime coauthor Mike Aquilina—takes up the task of reacquainting us with the flesh-and-blood Apostles and the dusty streets of the cities where they lived. It is designed as a companion volume to the television series *A.D.* Together, the book and the series can serve as a window on a place and time that is as important to our lives as our own childhood and infancy.

Jesus did not write books. But the Apostles did—and, as they did, they trained generations of Christians to read their way to deeper faith. I pray that readers of this book will experience the blessings of the apostolic Tradition on every page.

—Cardinal Donald Wuerl
Archbishop of Washington

Ministers and Martyrs

Introduction

Forget everything you know about the Apostles. Flush out of your mind whatever you have heard about the early Christians.

That's the first thing you have to do if you want to meet the real Apostles.

Here's the problem: We have almost two thousand years of tradition between us and the early Christians. And it's a glorious tradition, full of some of the deepest thoughts, the most beautiful art, the most soul-stirring music humanity has ever produced.

In that time we've developed a whole sacred language to describe every aspect of Christianity. *Minister*, *martyr*, *bishop*, *liturgy*, *Eucharist*—these are technical terms that people in the religion business use. Most of the rest of us have only a vague idea of what they mean.

The technical meanings, the long tradition, the glorious art—none of that was there when the Apostles and the people who knew them were first trying to figure out what it meant to follow Jesus. Instead, they told their stories and talked about what they meant in the ordinary language that everyone understood. And we have to get back to that if we're going to understand who these people we call Apostles really were, and what it was like to be them.

* * *

St. Peter's Basilica in Rome is the grandest, the biggest, and the most splendid church in the world. Some of the greatest architectural talent in European history was enlisted to design the building—Bramante, Michelangelo, Bernini. The number of priceless works of art in and around it is incalculable.

Walk through the nave toward the altar. Painted decorations fill every available space. Statues by the masters of Renaissance sculpture look down on you. Carved arches with details picked out in gold leaf glimmer in the shifting light from the vast dome ahead. Before you is a magnificent baldachin—a ceremonial canopy—that towers over the main altar. All this magnificence points to that altar. Everything in the building leads your eye to that central spot.

And under the altar lie the bones of St. Peter.

The whole basilica, with its arches and columns and statues and dome, is a reliquary for the decayed body of one of the Twelve Apostles.

And who was Peter?

He was some guy in a boat.

When Jesus called him, Peter was a fisherman on the Sea of Galilee, a little lake in the back country of Palestine. He was an ordinary working man with a wife who probably thought he spent too much time thinking about stuff and not enough time bringing back the fish. He was nobody special: in fact, the New Testament goes out of its way to tell us how not special he was. It also goes out of its way to tell us he was a coward, a liar, a waffler, and perennial candidate for apostle most likely to make a royal mess of things if given half a chance.

It's hard to imagine a greater disparity than the contrast between Peter's absolute ordinariness and the magnificent basilica that towers over his bones.

But there's nothing wrong with this picture. It's as if Peter was the plain little seed that sprouted and bloomed a Roman masterpiece. The ordinary bones of an ordinary Galilean fisherman grew into St. Peter's Basilica, because for all these centuries people have remembered what that ordinary fisherman did and what it led to.

We have to keep St. Peter's Basilica in mind when we go back in time to meet the Apostles and their friends.

We know that, over the course of two millennia, Christians have raised a glorious structure of thought and imagination on the humble foundation of a few ordinary working-class men and women from Palestine.

Yet all that glory came from the seeds those ordinary people planted. Like St. Peter's Basilica, our hallowed traditions, our art, our music, and our deepest thoughts of the past two thousand years all rest on the bones of real people who lived real lives.

* * *

Just like the people, the words we use to describe them started out as ordinary working-class words—the kind of words you would have used every day and never expected to amount to much. And just as archaeologists dig through the accumulated developments of centuries to find the truth about history, we can dig through the layers of later meanings to perform an archaeology of words.

Ministers and *martyrs*: these words have particular meanings to Christians. They're technical terms in our lexicon. But they come from ordinary words for ordinary, everyday things. The words have become encrusted with generations of theological interpretation and argument. They have been diminished through translation and the migration and development of cultures. But if we go back to the original ordinary senses of both words, we can encounter them afresh. We can see what they have to tell us about the first Christians and their world.

Let's start with *martyr*. The word *martyr* is Greek for "witness." A witness gives testimony in court, which is exactly what Christians had to do when their religion was an illegal cult. In those days, a hostile witness would often be tortured to make him tell the truth. (It worked about as well then as it does now.) So Jesus tells his followers:

> Beware of men; for they will deliver you up to councils, and flog you in their synagogues, and you will be dragged before governors and kings for my sake, to bear testimony before them and the Gentiles. (Matt. 10:17–18)

Testimony is *martyrion* in Greek. That's the ordinary use of the word: a *martyr* was someone who gave *testimony* in court.

And what should a Christian do in court? Jesus goes on:

> When they deliver you up, do not be anxious how you are to speak or what you are to say; for what you are to say will be given to you in that hour; for it is not you who speak, but the Spirit of your Father speaking through you. (Matt. 10:19–20)

When a Christian has to be a *witness*, the Holy Spirit will go to work and make the witnessing count. Already we see that, for a Christian, the ordinary act of giving testimony is taking on a supernatural meaning. The word *martyrion* means the same thing to a Christian that it means to any other ordinary Greek-speaking person. But because it's being done for Jesus' sake, and because Christ promises the help of the Holy Spirit, it means something more as well.

Jesus warns his followers that there may be a heavy price to pay:

> Brother will deliver up brother to death, and the father his child, and children will rise against parents and have them put to death; and you will be hated by all for my name's sake. But he who endures to the end will be saved. (Matt. 10:21–22)

Being a witness for Christ might have fatal consequences. There will be people who will die for their *martyrion*—their testimony.

And how about *minister*?

Minister has become a technical term in religion and politics. Protestants of certain sorts have adopted the word *minister* to mean the leader of a congregation. Parliamentary governments use *minister* to mean someone in charge of a ministry—a section of the government.

The English word *minister* comes from a Latin word that means "servant." It was an employee, someone paid (or, in the case of a slave, bought) to do a job. In Greek the word was *leitourgos*, and what he did was a *leitourgia*, from which we get another Christian technical term, *liturgy*. *Leitourgia* was a perfectly ordinary word for public works. The man who got stuck running the sewer commission was a *leitourgos*. Road building was a *leitourgia*.

And so was worship.

Life was not compartmentalized into the sacred and the secular. Religious duties were things that had to be done, just as much as building roads. The Hebrew word *abodah* meant the same thing, and it was usually translated into Greek as *leitourgia*. So, for example, when the Israelites had to make bricks for the Egyptians, that was *abodah*, or *leitourgia*. It certainly wasn't anything glamorous.

It was natural for Christians to adopt the usual language for their own people who got things done, and their own things that needed to be done. The term *liturgy* meant the community worship that Christians did together, and a minister—a *leitourgos*—was the person who led that community worship.

Just like giving testimony for Christ, though, there was that added supernatural dimension to the role of the minister. The minister was doing an everyday job, but the coming of Christ had infused the everyday with holiness. The bread and wine in the Christian liturgy was the Body and Blood of Christ, offered as a sacrifice for sin. Christ himself is the high priest who offers that sacrifice, but the minister participates in the offering. The Christian ministry was a sacrificial office, like the work of the priests in the Jewish Temple.

Since the minister was the most visible member of the community, he was more likely than anyone else to be hauled into court. A minister would often have to be a witness. And when Christianity was illegal, a witness would often have to die.

Bearing witness until death was the ultimate *sacrifice* that a minister could make—sacrifice not in the modern sense of giving up something that you'd rather hold on to, but in the original sense of *making holy* (that's what the Latin-derived word *sacrifice* means). His blood would be shed for Christ, and thus he would be sharing in Christ's own sacrifice. And that was cause for rejoicing. "Even if I am to be poured as a libation upon the sacrificial offering of your faith, I am glad and rejoice with you all," wrote St. Paul (Phil. 2:17). It was the complete fulfillment of the minister's work, the ultimate liturgy.

Ministers and *martyrs*—two very ordinary terms, but infused with deeper meaning by Christ.

* * *

This is the story we'll see repeated over and over again. The most ordinary words grow deep and subtle layers of meaning. The most ordinary things become rich with holy associations. The most ordinary people become the most extraordinary heroes.

Peter was a man who had denied Christ three times, by turns impulsive and cowardly. What gave him the strength to lead the young Christian Church?

Thomas was a congenital pessimist who refused to believe that Jesus was alive. What gave him the faith to carry the Christian message to far-off India?

Paul was a proud Pharisee who devoted all his energy to stamping out the Christian heresy. What turned him into the new sect's most zealous promoter?

It's easy to lose sight of the original ordinariness of the Apostles and their world. We see St. Peter in an icon, his expression firm but peaceful, his halo correctly in place. We see him as a statue, holding his key to heaven and gazing down on us with quiet dignity. We seldom see him outside the high priest's house, weeping bitterly because he has denied his Master.

But when we know that the Apostles were ordinary men, the real magnitude of what they accomplished comes into focus. When we remember that they lived in an ordinary world of smelly cities and dusty highways, we can see that there was something more than ordinary going on. A radiance shines through the stench of the city. The Holy Spirit is at work, turning the ordinary into the divine.

To know the first Christians as they really were, then, we need to visit them where they lived, in a particular place, at a particular time—a place and time where God had entered history as a man named Jesus of Nazareth.

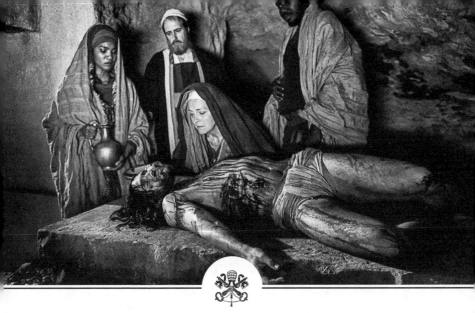

CHAPTER 1
Foundation Stones

*Then he opened their minds to understand the Scriptures,
and said to them, "Thus it is written, that the Christ should
suffer and on the third day rise from the dead, and that
repentance and forgiveness of sins should be preached in
his name to all nations, beginning from Jerusalem."*

—Luke 24:45–47

Salvation came to the humanity in a particular place, and it
went out to the world from that place: Jerusalem.

Christianity, from the beginning, was not a theory to
be found in books or a myth that yielded a moral. It had a
street address. The foundations of biblical religion could be
located in particular events in particular places, in actions
perpetrated by real people and recorded by eyewitnesses. For

Christians, said the historian Herbert Butterfield, "religious thought is inextricably involved in historical thought." Christianity "presents us with religious doctrines which are at the same time historical events or historical interpretations."[1]

Many religions of the ancient world promised salvation; but they couched it in allegories—myths that were patently fictitious but designed to engage the imagination, the mind, or the physical senses. Some of these religions were new on the scene, but they projected their origins on a distant past, lost to memory.

Only Christianity—and the Israelite religion from which it came—dared to present salvation in a way that was quite recent and historically verifiable. At the end of the first century, the Roman emperor Domitian, anxious about potential rivals, summoned the remaining relatives of Jesus, whose followers called him King of Kings. They were easily rounded up and interrogated. But Domitian found them laughably working-class, with calluses on their hands, and without much money or land to show for their labors; so he let them go.[2]

Christianity could be called up and examined. Its origins could be visited and investigated. One of the early pagan critics of the Church, a philosopher named Celsus, derided Christian claims—not because they were historically unsound, but because he could not imagine a god mucking about in a second-rate city like Jerusalem. It was high comedy to imagine

---

[1] Herbert Butterfield, *Christianity and History* (New York: Scribner, 1950), 3.
[2] The event is recorded by Hegesippus and Tertullian in the second century. Both sources can be found in Eusebius, *History of the Church*, 1.20.

a god born of a common woman who sewed her own clothing—a god who then called slaves, women, and children to be his followers. Celsus's response was typical. The Roman historians registered the rise of Christianity only in passing, and they dismissed it as insignificant.

If Christians had simply wanted to make an impression in the Greco-Roman world, they would have chosen terms other than those presented in the Gospels. But they could not recast the Gospel as a theory or a myth. Christianity was then, as it is today, accountable to history, and the earliest records testify to the lives and works of a carpenter turned rabbi, his fishermen disciples, and certain events that occurred during a Jewish holiday in a remote provincial capital.

* * *

The Israelites had always made extravagant claims about Jerusalem.

- It was the national capital established by King David, whose reign began a thousand years before the birth of Jesus.

- David's heir, Solomon, built an imposing Temple in Jerusalem. An architectural marvel it was, according to the Israelites, the only place on earth where sacrifice could be offered to their God—who was, they claimed, the only true God.

- David's royal house ruled from Jerusalem for centuries, but its golden age was very brief, lasting only through the reign of King Solomon. In the next generation, Israel's northern tribes seceded and established their own kingdom. Divided, the nation was weakened and subject to frequent attacks by the armies of neighboring countries. In time the north would fall to Assyrian invaders (722 B.C.), and the southern kingdom would be devastated and its inhabitants taken in captivity to Babylon (586 B.C.).

- Even then, however—when Jerusalem lay in rubble —the exiled Israelites still awaited the day when a descendant of David would reign in the city over the reunited tribes of Israel. That royal "Son of David" would be appointed by God and anointed for his historic role. He would rebuild the Temple and restore proper worship to the world. And he would rule not only Israel but all the nations.

Again, such claims surely seemed arrogant to outsiders. But Israel saw its vocation as singular and its future secured by the Creator of the world and Lord of history.

According to an ancient tradition, God had fashioned the world out of the stone that lay beneath the sanctuary of Jerusalem's Temple—and all the rest of the universe was "knit" from that colossal stone. The rabbis taught that the foundation stone, called the *eben shetiyah* in Hebrew, sealed away the forces of chaos and dissolution and thus preserved order in the world.[3]

---

[3] Traditions about the *Shetiyah* are numerous. They are well detailed in Louis Ginzberg, *The Legends of the Jews*, volume 1 (New York: Jewish Publication Society of America, 1909), 12. Ginzberg summarizes: "The construction of the earth was begun at the center, with the foundation stone of the Temple, the *Eben Shetiyah*, for the Holy Land is at the central point of

In the days of King Solomon, Israel's most sacred relic, the Ark of the Covenant, stood upon the *shetiyah*. Although the Ark disappeared at the time the first Temple was destroyed, during the Babylonian captivity, the *shetiyah* remained at the center of the rebuilt Temple. It was the site of the most solemn sacrifice each year, offered by the High Priest on the Day of Atonement, Yom Kippur.

Jerusalem, then, marked the center of the world. Everything else—not only in Jerusalem but in all creation—radiated outward from the foundation stone of the city's Temple.

The tribe of Judah, which was David's tribe, always maintained a presence in and around Jerusalem. From *Judah* came the name that foreigners gave to Israel's religion—Judaism. The people in the land were commonly known to their Greek-speaking neighbors as *Iudaioi*—which can be translated as Judeans, or Jews.

They awaited their royal savior, whom they called by the Hebrew word for "anointed one," *Moshiach* (*Messiah*), a word that the Greeks would translate as *Christos* and that we today render as *Christ*.

The Jews searched their Scriptures, especially the prophets, for clues to the Messiah's identity. He would be the Son of David. He would rule from Jerusalem. And the city would be made glorious in that day. The prophets spoke of the reign of

---

the surface of the earth, Jerusalem is at the central point of Palestine, and the Temple is situated at the center of the Holy City." See also Joseph Dan, "Jerusalem in Jewish Spirituality," in Nitza Rosovsky, ed., *City of the Great King: Jerusalem from David to the Present* (Cambridge: Harvard University Press, 1996), 64.

the Christ, or perhaps the Christ himself, in terms of a new foundation stone laid upon Zion, King David's mountain.

> Behold, I am laying in Zion for a
>   foundation
> a stone, a tested stone,
> a precious cornerstone, of a sure
>   foundation. (Isa. 28:16)

This would be good news not only for the tribes of Israel but for all the foreign nations as well—those who lived in the darkness of idolatry, without God's revelation.

The prophet Isaiah foretold that in the days of the Messiah they, too, would come to know God's law and share in true worship.

> It shall come to pass in the latter days
> that the mountain of the house of the
>   LORD
> shall be established as the highest of
>   the mountains,
> and shall be raised above the hills;
> and all the nations shall flow to it,
> and many peoples shall come, and say:
> "Come, let us go up to the mountain of
>   the LORD,
> to the house of the God of Jacob;
> that he may teach us his ways
> and that we may walk in his paths."
> For out of Zion shall go forth the law,
> and the word of the LORD from
>   Jerusalem. (Isa. 2:2–3)

* * *

Such were the hopes in Jerusalem when Jesus appeared. The Jews who lived there had an exalted sense of their city and its role in the drama of creation and history. All those expectations would be fulfilled, justified, and surpassed in the life of Jesus Christ—although surely not in the way most people expected.

The Roman province of Palestine included much of the territory God had long ago promised to the patriarch Abraham—the land his descendants occupied after their exodus from slavery in Egypt. Its history was full of conflict, occupation, and exile. In the centuries immediately before Christ, the Jews endured the oppression of Greek overlords who tried to enforce pagan practices, even in the Jerusalem Temple.

The Jews rebelled and prevailed against all odds and briefly sustained an uneasy self-rule. But this ceased when Rome, then an unstoppable world power, seized the lands in 63 B.C. The Roman general Pompey, on entering the city, profaned the Temple by entering the innermost sanctuary, the Holy of Holies.

Roman taxation was burdensome, and its military presence—rife with pagan symbols and practices—was offensive to the Jews. But Rome did strive to achieve peace through accommodation, installing local rulers who were more tolerant of Jewish practice. The king at the time of Jesus' birth, now known as Herod the Great, had mixed ancestry; he was an Edomite, but he observed Jewish ritual law and undertook the reconstruction and expansion of the Temple. The new edifice, which was still under construction at the time of Jesus' death, would be even grander than Solomon's original.

These new assertions of Jewish religious and national identity gave many people hope that the time of the Messiah was near. The New Testament mentions two ill-fated men who laid claim to the title and gathered a crowd of followers.

> For before these days Theudas arose, giving himself out to be somebody, and a number of men, about four hundred, joined him; but he was slain and all who followed him were dispersed and came to nothing. After him Judas the Galilean arose in the days of the census and drew away some of the people after him; he also perished, and all who followed him were scattered. (Acts 5:36–37)

The first-century Jewish historian Flavius Josephus confirms those two instances and adds still others.[4] Failed messiahs, however, were a passing excitement. There was great diversity in Jewish thought in the first century, but most of it coalesced around three major groups: Pharisees, Sadducees, and Essenes.[5] Josephus spelled out their differences for us,[6] though some of the distinctions are apparent from the New Testament as well.

---

[4] For Theudas and Judas, see Josephus, *Antiquities of the Jews* 20.97–98 and 18.1. For other would-be messiahs, see 17.10.6–7.

[5] For accessible modern descriptions of these groups, see James C. VanderKam, *An Introduction to Early Judaism* (Grand Rapids, MI: Eerdmans, 2001), 186–192; Jacob Neusner, *Judaism in the Beginning of Christianity* (Philadelphia: Fortress Press, 1984), 25–28; Günter Stemberger, *Jewish Contemporaries of Jesus: Pharisees, Sadducees, Essenes* (Minneapolis, MN: Fortress, 1995); and Stephen M. Wylen, *The Jews in the Time of Jesus: An Introduction* (Mahwah, NJ: Paulist, 1996), 133–147.

[6] Josephus, *Jewish War* 13.5.

- *Pharisees.* The name, from the Hebrew *parushim*, means "separatists." A lay movement, the Pharisees considered themselves to be guardians of an oral law passed down from the time of Moses—traditions that applied the Temple's ritual law to everyday life in the home and workplace. They sought to have all Israel living in ritual purity, keeping a strict kosher diet and cleansing their hands and dishware according to prescribed methods. They kept themselves separate from foreigners (Gentiles) and would not share meals with them. The Pharisees held strong beliefs in spiritual realities: the immortal soul, the existence of angels, God's providence, human freedom, the future resurrection of the righteous, and the eternal punishment of evildoers. Although they probably never numbered more than a few thousand, they were widely respected for their piety and were influential among the people. Pharisees appear often in the New Testament as opponents of Jesus and, later, of the Apostles. Before his conversion, St. Paul was a member of the Pharisee party (Acts 26:5; Phil. 3:5).

- *Sadducees.* If the Pharisees held the admiration of the common people, the Sadducees held control of the establishment. They were wealthy men and priests of high social status, who oversaw the ritual worship at the Jerusalem Temple. They emphasized the authority of Scripture (and perhaps only the first five books, the *Torah*), and they rejected the Pharisees' notion of an oral law. According to the New Testament, the Sadducees also denied the existence of an afterlife, angels, or other spirits (Acts 23:8). Their name seems to be derived from *Zadok*, the name of a priest at the time of King David. Thus, they associated themselves with the Temple's most ancient origins. Little else is known about the Sadducees' beliefs, as none of their own writings have survived. When the Romans destroyed the Jerusalem Temple in A.D. 70, the Sadducees lost their seat of power and vanished from the historical scene.

- *Essenes*. This third group, perhaps the smallest in number, emphasized personal discipline and close community. The Essenes lived simply and unostentatiously, holding all property in common. They revered priesthood and observed rigid distinctions between clergy and lay members. Some—and perhaps many—lived celibate lives. Some Essenes lived together in desert communes, similar in significant ways to Christian monasteries. Others lived in ordinary villages. They committed themselves to a strict regimen that ordered their daily lives. They studied Scripture deeply and observed a distinctive ritual life. Many scholars believe that the Dead Sea Scrolls, an ancient library unearthed in the middle of the twentieth century, were produced by an Essene community. The meaning of their name is uncertain. The Essenes first emerged in the centuries immediately before Christ. The First Book of Maccabees may record their beginnings: "Then many who were seeking righteousness and justice went down to the wilderness to dwell there" (1 Macc. 2:29). At the time of Jesus, the Essenes also had a community on Mount Zion in Jerusalem. For various reasons, they considered the contemporary Temple priesthood to be illegitimate; and so they refused to take part in its sacrifices, and they observed their own calendar of festivals. Since many of Jesus' distinctive practices, including celibacy, were similar to those of the Essenes, some scholars have proposed that his family was somehow connected with the Essenes.[7]

We know that there were factions even within these groups, and that there were many other, smaller movements. (One of twelve leaders Jesus chose is identified as a member of the Zealot party, which recognized no authority but God's.) As Jewish opposition to Rome became more radicalized, there arose extremist cells that today we would describe as terrorists. Josephus mentions several sects that sought to oppose any Gentile authority with violence. The New Testament describes a group that "made a plot and bound themselves by an oath neither to eat nor drink till they had killed" the Apostle Paul (Acts 23:12). Such radical groups multiplied and mutated as the first century wore on and Jews edged toward rebellion

[7] See Elizabeth McNamer and Bargil Pixner, *Jesus and First-Century Christianity in Jerusalem* (Mahwah, NJ: Paulist, 2008); Bargil Pixner. "Jesus and His Community: between Essenes and Pharisees," in J.H. Charlesworth and Loren L. Johns, eds., *Hillel and Jesus: Comparative Studies of Two Major Religious Leaders* (Minneapolis, MN: Fortress, 1997), 193–224; and Rainer Riesner, "Jesus, the Primitive Community, and the Essene Quarter of Jerusalem," in J.H. Charlesworth, *Jesus and the Dead Sea Scrolls* (New York: Doubleday, 1993), 198–234.

against their Roman overlords. The rebels were defeated as much by their own sectarian differences as by the force of Roman power.

In Jerusalem, religious dispute could be contentious and occasionally violent—as even this brief treatment makes clear. Religious questions, moreover, were not relegated to abstract considerations of theology. Jewish law regulated all aspects of life: diet, commerce, rest and leisure, family relations, and the limits of interaction with non-Jews.

Religious leaders, from many of the factions and sects, held positions in local and regional governance, which operated under careful Roman oversight. The kings in Herod's line tended at least to make a show of following Jewish law. In Jerusalem there was a governing council, called the Sanhedrin, that included religious scholars and chief priests. They convened to decide applications of Jewish law and pass judgment on possible violations. Their power was limited—they could not impose capital punishment—but, as the New Testament makes clear, the Sanhedrin could influence both Roman leaders (John 11:47-53 and 18:35) and Jerusalem mobs (Acts 6:8-7:60) to execute men it deemed to be criminals.

* * *

There are many fascinating characters in the drama that played out in Jerusalem that Passover weekend. It seems likely that many of them believed their actions and decisions were of historic or even cosmic importance. For those with a vested interest in the temporal order, too, religious questions could have social and professional consequences.

The rabbi Jesus had traveled the province for three years and consistently drawn crowds numbering in the thousands.

If Josephus is accurate in his census of the Pharisees, Saddu-cees, and Essenes, each of these movements numbered no more than a few thousand. Any one of Jesus' congregations might outnumber the total population of any two of the three major religious movements. In a matter of a few years, Jesus had managed to eclipse movements that had been active for a century or more. We should not be surprised to learn that groups usually opposed to one another, such as the Pharisees and Sadducees, managed to unite in their opposition to Jesus (see John 7:32, 45).

Many people who heard Jesus speak took the further step of declaring themselves to be his followers, or disciples. From these he selected twelve to be leaders. He invested them with authority that was extraordinary: "Truly, I say to you, whatever you bind on earth shall be bound in heaven, and whatever you loose on earth shall be loosed in heaven" (Matt. 18:18). They were to exercise this authority not just among them-selves, he said, but in the *ekklesia*—a word we translate today as "Church." Among Greek-speaking Jews of Jesus' time, how-ever, the word stood for the assembly of all Israel. This, too, must have seemed an extravagant claim for any rabbi to make, never mind one who had only recently arrived from the back-waters of Galilee.

Still, his words and deeds made many people wonder whether he might be the Messiah. In his dialogue with one of the Twelve, we can see that Jesus was already the subject of much speculation.

> Now when Jesus came into the district of Caesarea
> Philippi, he asked his disciples, "Who do men say that
> the Son of man is?"

And they said, "Some say John the Baptist, others say Elijah, and others Jeremiah or one of the prophets."

He said to them, "But who do you say that I am?"

Simon Peter replied, "You are the Christ, the Son of the living God."

And Jesus answered him, "Blessed are you, Simon Bar-Jona! For flesh and blood has not revealed this to you, but my Father who is in heaven. And I tell you, you are Peter, and on this rock I will build my Church, and the powers of death shall not prevail against it. I will give you the keys of the kingdom of heaven, and whatever you bind on earth shall be bound in heaven, and whatever you loose on earth shall be loosed in heaven."

Then he strictly charged the disciples to tell no one that he was the Christ. (Matt. 16:13–20)

Simon made the boldest possible statement about Jesus' identity, proclaiming him to be not merely the Messiah ("Christ") but also divine ("Son of the living God"). Others had guessed that Jesus was a deceased celebrity making a miraculous comeback. Simon saw that something far greater was happening: God was living among his people.

Jesus confirms Simon's profession of faith as he blesses him and gives him a new name—just as God had given a new name to the patriarch Abram (Gen. 17:5).

With Simon's new name came great authority and power. He would be the "rock" foundation of the new "assembly" of God's people, the Church.

Jesus, it seems, is establishing a new people, a new Jerusalem, a new Temple—even a new creation. All of these conclusions would eventually emerge in the writings of the Apostles.

As with the first creation, this new world, its city and its sanctuary, would rise from a foundation stone laid by God.

This time it would be a "living stone" (see 1 Pet. 2:5).

* * *

Simon Peter's authority is like that of the other eleven who would eventually be called Apostles. The power Jesus had first given to Simon—binding and loosing—he later gave to the others collectively. Peter is, in that sense, representative of the others; and, indeed, he often acts as their representative. It is Peter who usually asks the questions preoccupying everyone. Peter asks Jesus for clarification (Matt. 15:15). Peter dares to wonder what's in it for Jesus' followers: "Lo, we have left everything and followed you. What then shall we have?" (Matt. 19:27). When Jesus addresses a question to the Twelve generally, Peter responds for the group.

> Jesus said to the twelve, "Do you also wish to go away?"
> Simon Peter answered him, "Lord, to whom shall we go? You have the words of eternal life." (John 6:67–68)

Simon Peter is one among Twelve, yet he is also unique. At Jesus' bidding, he becomes the Master's vicar and shares the Master's life. Peter alone is called to walk on water with Jesus (Matt. 14:28–30). He alone joins Jesus in exemption from the half-shekel tax (Matt. 17:24–27). Peter alone is given the keys of the kingdom (Matt. 16:19)—keys symbolic of the power that the king of Israel shared with his prime minister (Isa. 22:20–22). At the end of his life, Peter would "glorify God" by the same manner of death that Jesus suffered (John 21:18–19).

Even in renaming Simon as "Rock" Jesus was sharing a quality proper to himself as Messiah. The earliest prediction of the Savior had referred to him as "the Mighty One ... the Shepherd, the Rock of Israel" (Gen. 49:24). Jesus was, according to his own testimony, the stone "the builders rejected," which became the cornerstone (Luke 20:17).

As Jesus' mission came to its climactic end, Peter played a pivotal role. He abandoned Jesus and denied him three times. His fall was spectacular: the man named prince of the Apostles fled in his Master's hour of need. Because of this, however, Simon Peter would later become a model of reconciliation with Christ (John 21:15–17).

He was an unlikely candidate for the position; and the name seems ill suited to him. A rock is steady and unchanging, but Peter could be impetuous and even violent (John 18:10). He was given to sudden enthusiasm and just-as-sudden loss of interest. He took a few steps on the water and then lost his nerve and began to sink. He insisted that Jesus must not wash his feet—and then insisted that Jesus wash his head and hands as well (John 13:6–9). He said he would never deny the Master, but then he did, repeatedly.

Nevertheless, it was Simon—not James, not John, not Judas—whom Jesus named as the Church's foundation stone.

And it was Simon Peter the Church spontaneously recognized as the Master's vicar, after Jesus had ascended into heaven. In the only surviving history of that period, the Acts of the Apostles, Peter is portrayed as the supreme judge and teacher. He confidently guides the Church as it transitions into a new generation. He is both an administrator and a missionary. He has the gift of healing. He determines how Judas the traitor will be replaced. He brings the question of the inclusion of the Gentiles to its final resolution. Peter fulfilled those duties for many years after his Master ascended to heaven, more than thirty years, according to the most ancient tradition.

At the time Jesus commissioned Simon Peter, he said, "on this Rock I will build my Church." He stated it in the future tense. The building began in earnest, no doubt, with the drama of the last Passover Jesus spent on earth. To this day, Jesus, the Christ, continues to build his Church, on the same foundation stone.[8]

[8] There are many excellent studies of Simon Peter and his unique authority. Pope Benedict XVI devoted a series of his Wednesday audiences to a profound examination of Peter's life. These are collected in Pope Benedict XVI, *The Apostles: Illustrated Edition* (Huntington, IN: Our Sunday Visitor, 2008), 59–77. A helpful introduction to Peter's ministry is J. Michael Miller, C.S.B., *The Shepherd and the Rock: Origins, Development, and Mission of the Papacy* (Huntington, IN: Our Sunday Visitor, 1995). The Lutheran scholar Oscar Cullman grappled with the implications of Peter's authority in *Peter: Disciple, Apostle, Martyr* (New York: Meridian, 1958); his study is best read alongside the response by Catholic theologian (and future cardinal) Charles Journet, *The Primacy of Peter: From the Protestant and from the Catholic Point of View* (Westminster, MD: Newman, 1954).

CHAPTER 2
The Apostles: Those Who Are Sent

Modern readers tend to see the Gospel through a filter of tradition. We see individual characters as we have been trained to see them: as the sum of the sermons preached about them. The text may present them as complex, with a variety of competing virtues and failings, but our mental shorthand reduces them to a single quality.

Take Doubting Thomas. His memory (like his nickname) rests largely on a single scene near the end of the fourth Gospel. The scene begins with the disciples hiding behind locked doors (John 20:19). They were afraid. They had already received the news of Jesus' Resurrection, but still they dared not show their faces outside. The locks on the door presented no obstacle to the glorified body of the risen Jesus. He suddenly stood among the disciples. He blessed them, and he endowed them with power to forgive sins. All this took place, however, while Thomas was away.

> Now Thomas, one of the twelve, called the Twin, was not with them when Jesus came. So the other disciples told him, "We have seen the Lord." But he said to them, "Unless I see in his hands the print of the nails, and place my finger in the mark of the nails, and place my hand in his side, I will not believe."
>
> Eight days later, his disciples were again in the house, and Thomas was with them. The doors were shut, but Jesus came and stood among them, and said, "Peace be with you." Then he said to Thomas, "Put your finger here, and see my hands; and put out your hand, and place it in my side; do not be faithless, but believing." Thomas answered him, "My Lord and my God!" Jesus said to him, "Have you believed because you have seen me? Blessed are those who have not seen and yet believe." (John 20:24–29)

Perhaps Thomas can be forgiven for disbelieving his fellow disciples. They had hardly proven themselves reliable over that Passover holiday. They had all fled the Master—all except John, who, tradition tells us, was the youngest of them.

Thomas was indeed incredulous, and his retort had the same quirky combination of courage and pessimism that he had shown at other moments in Jesus' ministry. When the Master informed the Twelve that he would be going onward to Judea, Thomas said to the others: "Let us also go, that we may die with him" (John 11:16). On another occasion, when Jesus asked his disciples to follow after him, Thomas raised the obvious question that no one else dared to ask: "Lord, we do not know where you are going; how can we know the way?" To which Jesus replied: "I am the way, and the truth, and the life; no one comes to the Father, but by me" (John 14:5–6). Thomas was brooding and could be downbeat; and yet he managed to elicit some of Jesus' most stunning acts of self-revelation.

None was more stunning than Thomas's encounter with the risen Lord. Jesus did not merely identify himself—which would have been enough—but invited Thomas to make the most invasive verification: "Put your finger here ... put your hand in my side."

The moment bespoke an intimacy between Jesus and those chosen disciples. In the encounter we see a bond of fellowship and friendship all the more remarkable because those men had, only days before, abandoned Jesus when he was suffering.

* * *

They were first known as the Twelve—a numeral and a name laden with meaning. For a Jew of the first century, it recalled the twelve tribes of Israel, the tribes now dispersed among the Gentiles and assimilated into other peoples.

> Crush the heads of the rulers of the enemy,
>   who say, "There is no one but ourselves."
> Gather all the tribes of Jacob,
>   and give them their inheritance, as at the beginning.
> Have mercy, O Lord, upon the people called by thy
>   name,
>   upon Israel, whom thou hast likened to a first-born
>   son. (Sir. 36:10–12)

The gathering of the scattered was seen as an essential component of God's salvation. The reconstitution of Israel was a work expected of the Messiah, the Christ.

Jesus' choice of twelve leaders was symbolic and suggestive—even provocative. Clearly he sensed the gravity of the moment. He spent the preceding night in a vigil of intense prayer.

> In these days he went out to the mountain to pray; and all night he continued in prayer to God. And when it was day, he called his disciples, and chose from them twelve, whom he named Apostles; Simon, whom he named Peter, and Andrew his brother, and James and John, and Philip, and Bartholomew, and Matthew, and Thomas, and James the son of Alphaeus, and Simon who was called the Zealot, and Judas the son of James, and Judas Iscariot, who became a traitor. (Luke 6:12-16)

Biblical religion always involved a community—an assembly, in Hebrew, a *qahal*—and the community always observed a certain order. In the earliest days, the patriarchs served as priests within their tribes. Later, a single tribe exercised the priesthood. And later still, in the time of exile, when Temple sacrifice was impossible, the people met in synagogues to study the sacred books and pray.

It is possible that the authority Jesus established was based on an older tradition. The Essenes, for example, seem to have been governed by a council of twelve along with an inner circle of three priests and a supreme "presider" or "president."[9]

---

[9] Frank Moore Cross, *The Ancient Library of Qumran* (Minneapolis, MN: Fortress Press, 1995), 165–167.

Jesus chose his Twelve, but often called three of them—Peter, John, and James—apart at special times. Only the members of this inner circle witnessed Jesus' Transfiguration (Matt. 17:1–2); only they were permitted to witness certain miracles (see Mark 5:37–42); and only they were asked to accompany him in prayer in the Garden of Gethsemane (Mark 14:32). Over all of them, as we saw in the last chapter, stood Simon Peter. He appears first in every New Testament list of the Twelve.

It is unlikely that the Apostles themselves would have missed the significance of their number. Jesus himself stated it explicitly as he turns the kingdom over to them at his Last Supper:

> You are those who have continued with me in my trials; as my Father appointed a kingdom for me, so do I appoint for you that you may eat and drink at my table in my kingdom, and sit on thrones judging the twelve tribes of Israel. (Luke 22:28–30)

The Master followed this statement immediately with a special reassurance for the Apostle who held primacy: "Simon, Simon, behold, Satan demanded to have you, that he might sift you like wheat, but I have prayed for you that your faith may not fail; and when you have turned again, strengthen your brethren" (Luke 22:31–32).

The word *apostle* appears only rarely in the Gospels, where these men are usually called the Twelve. It is everywhere, however—beginning with the title—in the Acts of the Apostles and then appears frequently in the New Testament letters (which are all attributed to Apostles). The title is later extended, beyond the Twelve, to others. When Judas commits suicide, he is replaced by Matthias. Paul, a later convert, is called an Apostle.

And a missionary named Apollos is even called, with some degree of irony, a "super-Apostle" (cf. 2 Cor. 11:5).

The office was a phenomenon of that first generation. Never in the centuries that follow do we find men claiming the title of Apostle. Although the Church's bishops have always traced their authority to that of the Apostles, they have never used the title to describe themselves. Their authority is apostolic, but they themselves are not Apostles.

The title has a simple meaning. The Greek *apostolos* means "one who is sent." It describes an agent or vicar, an emissary or ambassador. More than a messenger, an *apostolos* is a representative. Scholars believe the word is a direct translation of the Hebrew *shaliah*; and the ancient rabbis pronounced that "a man's *shaliah* is as himself."[10]

As Jesus transferred authority and power to the Apostles, he compared the action to his own commissioning by God the Father: "As the Father has sent me, even so I send you" (John 20:21). As Jesus had acted in the power of the Holy Spirit, so he gave the Spirit in turn to his chosen men (John 20:22).

The office of Apostle was not something any of the Twelve had earned. They had, in fact, repeatedly proven themselves unworthy of the office and unprepared for the tasks. After years of instruction, they could still move their Teacher to exasperation: "Have I been with you so long, and yet you do not know me?" (John 14:9). In the face of danger, they had "scattered," running to their homes, leaving the Christ "alone" (John 16:32).

Yet he did not deny them the office he had already designated. Each Apostle would serve as his agent, his representative,

---

[10] *Mishnah Berakoth* 5:5.

his *shaliah*. Each would be as Jesus himself. Each would be empowered to do the things that Jesus himself had done: heal the sick, cast out demons, and raise the dead (see Acts 3:6–8; 5:16; 9:36–41). Jesus even gave them the means to perform an act reserved only to God; they could forgive sins (see John 20:23; cf. Mark 2:7).

St. Paul told the Corinthians that he forgave sins *en prosopo Christou*—which in the original Greek is a strong statement (2 Cor. 2:10). The word *prosopon* is multifaceted; it means "person," "presence," and "face." When the Apostle forgave, therefore, he was acting not in his own "person," but rather as Jesus' ongoing presence in the world. He was the Master's face to the world. As most of the historical Bible translations—from St. Jerome's Latin Vulgate to the King James Version—have made clear, the Apostle offered forgiveness "in the person of Christ."

A man's Apostle, after all, *is as himself.*

* * *

The Apostles themselves knew their unworthiness; but they also knew the dignity of their office. Paul spoke of the inner circle of Peter, John, and James as "pillars" of the Church (Gal. 2:9). The Twelve were the "foundation" Paul was building on, and Christ was the "cornerstone" (Eph. 2:20). In the book of Revelation, John sees the Twelve enshrined as foundation stones of the new and heavenly Jerusalem (Rev. 21:14).

Pillars and foundation stones, the Apostles were designated to hold the Church together and hold it up. So the ancient creeds spoke of the Church as "one, holy, catholic, and *apostolic*." The bestselling Christian books from the early centuries all bore titles that claimed a connection to the Church's original leadership: *The Apostolic Tradition*, *The Apostolic Constitutions*,

The Apostolic Teaching, Proof of the Apostolic Preaching. The Christian people shared a sense that no preaching, tradition, or doctrine was legitimate unless it could be traced to the generation of the Apostles.

It is remarkable—considering their failures recorded in the Gospels—to see the certainty and confidence with which the Apostles established the life that the Church would follow ever afterward. Some of them wrote pastoral letters that established patterns of discipline, order, and morals; and these ended up, eventually, among the sacred books of the Church. All of the Apostles, however, founded churches and established a distinctively Christian ritual life. Long before the New Testament books were written, the Church was already observing sacramental rites such as the washing of Baptism (Rom. 6:4), the "breaking of the bread" (Acts 2:42), the laying on of hands (2 Tim. 1:6), the confession of sins (James 5:16), the seal of the Holy Spirit (Acts 19:2), and the anointing of the sick (James 5:14).

The Apostles established the life of the Church as a "tradition," something "handed on" or "delivered" (1 Cor. 11:2, 23; 15:3)—something that the churches would have to hand on in turn. Fidelity to this tradition was a frequent concern of St. Paul: "So then, brethren, stand firm and hold to the traditions which you were taught by us, either by word of mouth or by letter" (2 Thess. 2:15). "Now we command you, brethren, in the name of our Lord Jesus Christ, that you keep away from any brother who is living in idleness and not in accord with the tradition that you received from us" (2 Thess. 3:6). "I commend you because you remember me in everything and maintain the traditions even as I have delivered them to you" (1 Cor. 11:2).

St. Paul considered himself a "steward of the mysteries of God" (cf. 1 Cor. 4:1). He was entrusted with authority, doctrine, and a way of life; and he was charged with communicating those "mysteries" to other people and other generations.

* * *

The Apostles were more than administrators in the Church, more than merely functionaries and overseers.

The word *apostle* itself has a dynamic quality. It denotes a sending, a mission, a movement outward. The Apostles' lives were marked by activity; their story is told, appropriately enough, in the book titled the *Acts* of the Apostles.

The word *Apostle* indicates a certain dynamism in the office and in the Church. The Church of Christ was not to be (as Israel had been) a reserve of purity, insulated from the world; it was rather an overflow of purity *into* the world, touching all the nations. As Jesus sent the Apostles forth on their mission, he said: "you shall be my witnesses in Jerusalem and in all Judea and Samaria and to the end of the earth" (Acts 1:8).

The New Testament tells some of the story of some of their travels. In the centuries immediately afterward, the earliest Christian historians set down the stories (and legends) of all of the Apostles' missionary journeys. Many of these were gathered together in books modeled after the New Testament's history: the *Acts of John*, *Acts of Peter*, *Acts of Paul*, and *Acts of Andrew*—all were likely set down before the year 200.[11]

---

[11] Two good popular works on the Apostles' labors are William Steuart McBirnie, *The Search for the Twelve Apostles* (Wheaton, IL: Tyndale House, 1973) and C. Bernard Ruffin, *The Twelve: The Lives of the Apostles after Calvary* (Huntington, IN: Our Sunday Visitor, 1998).

If these early accounts are to be trusted, perhaps no one carried out Jesus' command as literally as Doubting Thomas did. Jesus told his Apostles to be his witnesses "to the end of the earth," and all the early traditions agree that Thomas went to the limits of the known world: he brought the gospel to India. The testimony of this is consistent in the most ancient histories and the sermons and letters of the early Church Fathers. When Pantaenus, a second-century missionary, traveled from Egypt to India, he found the Church already established there. When later missionaries (and explorers such as Marco Polo) arrived, they found Christians who honored Thomas as their patron. For centuries, epic poems about Thomas were handed down not only in Christian families, but also in Hindu families![12]

Witness to India is a fitting end to the life of the man who dared to go abroad in Jerusalem in the days after Jesus' death.

It seems as if the earth itself—and human events—had conspired for centuries to make way for the *acts* of the Apostles.

---

[12] Many standard histories of India take Thomas's presence for granted. See, for example, Romila Thapar, *A History of India,* vol. 1 (Baltimore: Penguin Books, 1966). The most concise, sober, and judicious review of the evidence for Thomas's mission is in A.M. Mundadan, *History of Christianity in India* (Bangalore: CHAI, 2001). The most complete compilation of studies (for and against Thomas's historical presence in India) is George Menachery, ed., *The Nazranies* (Thiruvananthapuram, India: South Asia Research Assistance Services, 1998). Also helpful is Professor Menachery's *Thomapedia.* (Thiruvananthapuram, India: Saint Joseph's Press, 2000). A bibliography on the subject can be found in Mike Aquilina and Christopher Bailey, *The Doubter's Novena* (Huntington, IN: Our Sunday Visitor, 2010).

Such missions would have been difficult or impossible before Alexander the Great had opened up the Silk Road to the Far East and before the Romans had laid down thousands of miles of roads in the West.

Travel to India, in fact, was arduous until the time of Christ. It was right around then that Caesar Augustus suppressed piracy on the high seas. It was right around then that a sailor named Hippalus discovered the trade winds, enabling ships to travel on the open ocean from the Red Sea to the Indian peninsula.[13]

The world, it seems, was waiting for someone to be sent.

---

[13] See William H. Schoff, *The Periplus of the Erythraean Sea: Travel and Trade in the Indian Ocean by a Merchant of the First Century* (New York: Longmans, Green, and Co., 1912), 45–46.

CHAPTER 3

Pentecost:
The Church Is Born

Pentecost is the setting of the most spectacular scene in the historical books of the New Testament.

A sound came from heaven like the rush of a mighty wind. Tongues of fire appeared and rested on the disciples—but did not burn them! The men rushed into the streets and began to proclaim Jesus Christ before the multitude that had gathered in Jerusalem for the feast day.

The Holy Spirit arrived in a great show of power, attended by wonders and miracles, manifest before a cast of thousands.

Other miracles had taken place amid large crowds. On several occasions, Jesus had fed multitudes with just a few loaves and fishes—but the miracles themselves seem to have unfolded quietly, without thunder, wind, or flames. Jesus' walking on water had been eye-opening, but the witnesses then were few.

Pentecost was a singular event—unprecedented, although long foreshadowed; unique, although it would extend throughout subsequent history through the ministry of the Church.

* * *

Jerusalem's streets were crowded with pilgrims from all over the known world. Pentecost was the annual harvest festival of the Jews, and it was one of three feasts that all Jewish males were bound by law to observe in the holy city. The Lord God had said to Moses at Sinai: "Three times in the year you shall keep a feast to me.... Three times in the year shall all your males appear before the Lord" (Exod. 23:14–17).

The three days of obligation were Passover, Sukkot (known in English as the Feast of Booths or Tabernacles), and Pentecost. The name Pentecost came from the Greek word for "fiftieth" (*pentekostos*). In Jesus' time, the feast took place, for most Jews, on the fiftieth day after Passover.

In Hebrew the day was *Shavuot*, the Feast of Weeks, because it took place on the day following a "week of weeks"—seven times seven days—counting from Passover (Lev. 23:15–16). It was originally an agrarian festival, celebrating the beginning of the harvest season. God commanded through Moses: "You shall keep the feast of harvest, of the first fruits of your labor, of what you sow in the field" (Exod. 23:16). The feast was a ritual reminder that God was the source of Israel's blessings, and they owed their first and best of everything to him.

Over the centuries, Pentecost had grown in importance and had gathered layers of spiritual and historical significance.

By the lifetime of Jesus and the Apostles, it had become primarily a celebration of the giving of the law to Moses. As Passover recalled the Exodus from Egypt, so fifty days later the feast marked the great event at Mount Sinai: Moses received the law from God and renewed God's covenant with his chosen people (Exod. 24:7–8). Thus the Jews came, over time, to see Pentecost as a completion of Passover. What God had begun in Egypt, he sealed by giving the law.

Pentecost, then, was a celebration of the covenant, God's family bond with Israel. The *Book of Jubilees*, composed in the first centuries before Christ, claimed that Pentecost was the actual anniversary date not only of Moses' covenant at Sinai but also of God's covenants with Noah and with Abraham.[14] The Essenes, who were known for their emphasis on the covenant, made and renewed their religious commitments on that day.[15]

For Jews of the first century it was a great feast, a holy day of obligation. And those who lived in distant lands fulfilled their duty by traveling to Jerusalem. The city's population swelled, and there was a general feeling of festivity, of gratitude for all good gifts, from the Exodus and the Law to the abundance of the barley harvest.

* * *

The Apostles, meanwhile, were living in quiet expectation. They knew that something big was coming. Jesus had promised them as much when he took his leave from them.

---

[14] See *Book of Jubilees* 14:18–20.
[15] J.T. Milik, *Ten Years of Discovery in the Wilderness of Judaea* (Naperville, IL: Alec R. Allenson, 1959), 117–118.

He ... charged them not to depart from Jerusalem, but to wait for the promise of the Father, which, he said, "you heard from me, for John baptized with water, but before many days you shall be baptized with the Holy Spirit.... [Y]ou shall receive power when the Holy Spirit has come upon you." (Acts 1:4–5, 8)

They knew of the Holy Spirit from Jesus' promises at the Last Supper (John 14:16, 26). The Holy Spirit would be a "counselor" and a "consoler," sent by the Father, to "teach ... all things" and remind the Apostles of everything Jesus had said. The Holy Spirit would be with them forever.

It was a mysterious promise. When Jesus spoke of the Spirit, he seemed to be talking about a person—not simply a force or a grace—and that person seemed to be divine.

For forty days after Passover—forty days after his Resurrection—Jesus appeared to the Apostles and taught them. Yet he trained their gaze forward in time, as if his work was not yet done, as if his Passover awaited its completion.

After Jesus' Ascension, the Apostles returned to their room and, once again, locked themselves in. They attended to some practical matters; they selected a replacement for Judas. Most of all they prayed. St. Luke, the author of Acts, after listing the names of the Apostles, says: "All these with one accord devoted themselves to prayer, together with the women and Mary the mother of Jesus, and with his brethren" (Acts 1:14).

It is significant that the whole Church is with Mary as it waits to be "born" on Pentecost. Other than the Apostles, she is the only individual to be named. In Luke's other New Testament book, his Gospel, he repeatedly suggests that Mary served as a source of his historical information (see Luke

1:2; 2:19, 51). Her placement in this scene may serve a similar purpose.[16] It also establishes a neat parallel between Acts and Luke's Gospel, which opens as young Mary awaits the overshadowing of the Holy Spirit (see Luke 1:35). Luke, as a student of St. Paul, knew the Church to be the "body of Christ" (see 1 Cor. 12:27; Eph. 4:12). Just as Jesus' physical body was conceived by the power of the Holy Spirit and through the willing prayers of Mary, so his Mystical Body would be conceived in a similar way. Thus, Luke gives due notice to Mary's presence in the Upper Room in Jerusalem.

There is a quiet quality to the opening chapter of the Acts of the Apostles. The Apostles go about their business with solemnity, gravity, sobriety. They discuss Judas's sorrowful end. They lay down rules for succession in his "office" (Acts 1:20). They select Matthias as his successor, based on the criteria they had just established.

The tone is utterly prosaic and almost bureaucratic. While the first chapter of Acts reads almost like the minutes of a meeting, chapter 2 opens like the detonation of a bomb.

* * *

When the day of Pentecost had come, they were all together in one place. And suddenly a sound came from heaven like the rush of a mighty wind, and it filled all the house where they were sitting. And there appeared to them tongues as of fire, distributed and resting on

---

[16] Ancient traditions place both Luke and Mary in Ephesus for periods of time in the mid-first century. If the great historian of Jesus found himself in close proximity to the Mother of Jesus, there can be no doubt that he would pursue an interview.

each one of them. And they were all filled with the Holy Spirit and began to speak in other tongues, as the Spirit gave them utterance.

Now there were dwelling in Jerusalem Jews, devout men from every nation under heaven. And at this sound the multitude came together, and they were bewildered, because each one heard them speaking in his own language. And they were amazed and wondered, saying, "Are not all these who are speaking Galileans? And how is it that we hear, each of us in his own native language?" (Acts 2:1–8)

Perhaps the Apostles were expecting something to happen on the feast. They knew that Jesus, in his earthly ministry, had scrupulously observed the religious calendar and made his annual pilgrimages to Jerusalem, just as the law required. No matter what they expected, however, Pentecost surely exceeded it.

The cosmic phenomena, the wind and fire, would have been familiar because of the context of the feast day. They had been prefigured when God gave the law to Moses. In those days, "there were thunders and lightnings, and a thick cloud upon the mountain, and a very loud trumpet blast.... And Mount Sinai was wrapped in smoke" (Exod. 19:16, 18). Now, on the anniversary, came fire from heaven and a sound like the rush of a mighty wind.

Yet the "multitude" drew near not to see the spectacles but rather because the Apostles were speaking to their hearts. Jews had come to Jerusalem from all over the known world. There were

Parthians and Medes and Elamites and residents of Mesopotamia, Judea and Cappadocia, Pontus and Asia,

Phrygia and Pamphylia, Egypt and the parts of Libya belonging to Cyrene, and visitors from Rome, both Jews and proselytes, Cretans and Arabians. (Acts 2:9–11)

The list is orderly, running from east (Parthia) to West (Rome). The people present were ethnically Jews, but linguistically and culturally diverse. At that Pentecost, God made them all one people, even with their differences. The gift of the Holy Spirit was not that each heard the gospel in Hebrew, Aramaic, or Greek and understood it nonetheless, but that each heard "in his own native language." They were empowered, then, to take the gospel back to their places of origin.

In Luke's description of Pentecost, even the listings are rhetorically forceful—even the allusions to the Old Testament are resonant. Chapter 2 stands in stark contrast to chapter 1, where both the lists and the citations of the law seem muted.

Now there was action. Now there were arguments. The crowd grew as gawkers and scoffers joined the genuinely curious and the piously astonished. Some asked, "What does this mean?" Others said the meaning was simple: these men are drunk.

Just the day before, Peter had been speaking *sotto voce*. Now he stood and raised his voice to deliver a forceful sermon. He acknowledged the charges of drunkenness but only to dismiss them. Then he cut to the chase, quoting at length from the Old Testament prophet Joel:

> And in the last days it shall be, God declares,
> that I will pour out my Spirit upon all flesh,
> and your sons and your daughters shall
>   prophesy,
> and your young men shall see visions,

and your old men shall dream dreams;
yea, and on my menservants and my
    maidservants in those days
I will pour out my Spirit; and they shall
    prophesy. (Acts 2:17–18)

Peter described the "last days" in terms that were fulfilled that very day. The Spirit was indeed poured out, and the effects were visible in the streets of Jerusalem, noticed even by those who did not believe. This was the day the Lord had promised. From the moment of Pentecost forward, gifts once reserved to a few—such as prophecy—would now be distributed widely, from Parthia to Rome and beyond.

Peter drew from the heritage he held in common with his hearers. He quoted the prophet Joel and the psalms of David. He pointed to nearby monuments that would have been familiar to the pilgrims. He established his standing as a Jew among Jews; and then he called them, as Jews, to join him in repentance for any part they may have played in the Crucifixion of Jesus. This is not an anti-Jewish tirade, as some have portrayed it. Peter is speaking as the guiltiest man present, and he could not have conceived himself as anything but a Jew.

The urgency of his call was evident not only from his tone, but from the circumstances—the signs and wonders that recalled the giving of the law. It should come as no surprise, then, that many found his case compelling. "What shall we do?" they asked (Acts 2:37).

And Peter said to them: "Repent, and be baptized every one of you in the name of Jesus Christ for the forgiveness of your sins; *and you shall receive the gift of the Holy Spirit*" (Acts 2:38, emphasis added). This is the message that would always be associated with Peter. Salvation is, by definition, the gift of the Holy Spirit (1 Pet. 1:2); and Baptism "now saves you" (1 Pet. 3:21).

Peter extended the invitation not only to his hearers but to their households as well—"your children"—and to their loved ones still in their native lands. It was a remarkable offer. At least three thousand people, St. Luke tells us, took up the invitation and were baptized on that first Christian Pentecost.

It was not yet evident that this salvation would be extended to non-Jews. But the means were now in place for the message to extend to the farthest reaches of the earth. It would be universal in scope. It would be catholic in its reach. From its birth the Church was one. It was holy with the holiness of God, suffused by the Spirit. It was patently catholic, and it was undeniably apostolic.

* * *

The Church had a form, from the very beginning. In his book-length study *Open to the Holy Spirit*, Cardinal Donald Wuerl observes:

> Sometimes the Christian Pentecost is portrayed as a wild, anarchic event, producing a kind of cheerful chaos—a riot of movement with no discernible order. That was indeed the conclusion of the cynical onlookers—those who stood at a safe distance that day in Jerusalem, and who concluded that the Apostles were drunk on new wine. But it does not represent the perspective of faith.[17]

[17] Cardinal Donald Wuerl, *Open to the Holy Spirit: Living the Gospel with Wisdom and Power* (Huntington, IN: Our Sunday Visitor, 2014), 40.

On Pentecost, the Church was born with an unprecedented degree of freedom. As God had once given the law to Moses, so now he gave his own Spirit to the Church. The Spirit was manifest in unexpected prodigies and *charisms* (from the Greek word for "gifts")—such as speaking in diverse tongues and understanding those tongues. Mere men were entrusted with the means of salvation, a divine action. Yet among those charisms was the gift of leadership, *authority*. It is significant that not everyone preached on the first Pentecost; not everyone led; not everyone taught; not everyone issued the call to repentance. Peter did; the Apostles did. They fulfilled the roles of the office they had been given by Jesus.

The Church, from the beginning, had a hierarchy, a sacred order, although that order would develop further over time. The order of deacons, for example, would appear later in the book of Acts (6:3–6), as would the office of elder, or presbyter (20:17, 18). Over the next century, the roles of each office would become clearer as the Church grew. By the beginning of the second century, St. Ignatius of Antioch could write to far-flung churches and assume that each had a three-tiered hierarchy of bishop, presbyter, and deacon; and each gathered regularly, as the Apostolic Church did, for the Eucharist (Acts 2:42).

* * *

The Apostles had already been commissioned to do what Jesus had done, and do it all in the name of God. Now they were empowered to do so. Every person baptized that day received, to some degree, a share in the Apostles' mission—for they received a share in the life of Jesus Christ. In Baptism they became "partakers of the divine nature" (2 Pet. 1:4).

One of the great preachers of the early Church, St. John Chrysostom, identified this as the difference made at Pentecost: a tongue of heavenly fire had been added to human nature. Salvation now was nothing less than the sharing of divine life with all those who believed in Jesus Christ and were baptized—all three thousand on that first day.

Some years before Jesus had said to his disciples, "The harvest is plentiful" (Luke 10:2). The great harvest began, appropriately enough, at Pentecost, the feast of the harvest—the day dedicated to the gathering and offering of firstfruits.

At every level, the ancient feast found fulfillment that day in Jerusalem. The harvest was in. The new Passover reached its completion. The new exodus brought a renewed Israel to receive the new law—the Spirit of God—and now the New Covenant would extend to the very ends of the earth.

This would be the task not of scholars or financiers, not of armies or kings, but of rough men with limited abilities. Even in this detail, the story follows the pattern of God's choices. Moses himself was halting of speech. David was the unimposing and least likely among a large brood of brothers to be made a king. The Apostles received the divine power of the Holy Spirit to accomplish the work Christ had assigned them. They succeeded.

The first book of the Bible told the story of how the people of the earth became *peoples* opposed to one another. It is the story of the Tower of Babel (Gen. 11:1–9). All subsequent history followed the same narrative of endless division. Pentecost, however, reversed the process, repaired the breaches, restored broken bonds, and gathered the firstfruits—the tribes of Israel from their dispersion. Soon salvation would go out to the nations, the Gentiles, as well.

The gift of Pentecost would be extended to every believer through the ministry of the Church. The Apostles Peter and John traveled from Judea to Samaria, where a number of believers were eager for the gift. "Then they laid their hands on them and they received the Holy Spirit" (Acts 8:14–17).

This remains the story of the Church in every age. In the third century, an Egyptian Scripture scholar named Origen said that Pentecost is the feast most characteristic of Christian life. The true Christian, he said, "is always living in the season of Pentecost."[18]

[18] Origen, *Against Celsus* 8.22.

CHAPTER 4

A New Revelation of God

In many places throughout the world, Christians observe Pentecost Sunday as a celebration of God as the Trinity—three divine Persons living eternally in perfect unity: Father, Son, and Holy Spirit. The Trinity is the mystery at the heart of Christianity, and from the beginning it distinguished the apostolic Faith from everything else. It is the foundation of every Christian creed; all other dogmas, all other revelation, come from the fact that God is three in one.

The Apostles preached, insistently, that "God is one." St. Paul said it plainly (Rom. 3:30; 1 Cor. 8:4–6; Gal. 3:20), as did St. James (James 2:19). In the entire New Testament, there is nothing to suggest a second god—a god besides God.

The Apostles' monotheism was continuous with their religious heritage. God had said through the prophet Isaiah: "I am the LORD, and there is no other, besides me there is no God" (Isa. 45:5). And, in the time of Jesus, Jews daily recalled the words of Moses: "Hear, O Israel: The LORD our God is one LORD; and you shall love the LORD your God with all your heart, and with all your soul, and with all your might" (Deut. 6:4–5). The God preached by the Apostles is one, and he demanded a total and undivided commitment from anyone who would enter his covenant.

Yet from the first day of the Church's life, it was clear that the one God is also three. As Peter preached his first public sermon, he spoke of the Father, the Son, and the Spirit: "Being therefore exalted at the right hand of God, and having received from the Father the promise of the Holy Spirit, [Jesus] has poured out this which you see and hear" (Acts 2:33).

The God Peter preached was not a solitary being, but an eternal communion. The God revealed on Pentecost was interpersonal. Only of such a deity could the Apostles say: "God is love" (1 John 4:8, 16).

* * *

The Apostles grounded this most fundamental belief in a revelation given by Jesus himself. In the last sentence recorded in St. Matthew's Gospel, Jesus instructed his disciples to baptize "in the name of the Father and of the Son and of the Holy Spirit" (Matt. 28:19). They were to act in one divine "name" that clearly applied to three distinct persons. Father, Son, and Spirit share the "name" of God equally. Jesus' Great Commission, then, was the immediate background for Peter's first proclamation.

But even before the Great Commission, Jesus had spoken of himself as "one" with the Father (John 10:30). The being of the Father and Son, he said, was relational and inseparable: "the Father is in me, and I am in the Father" (John 10:38). As God had revealed himself to Moses by the name "I AM" (Exod. 3:14), so Jesus claimed that name as his own. "Truly, truly, I say to you, before Abraham was, I AM" (John 8:58). Only immortal, eternal God could make such a statement.

Nevertheless, Jesus was clearly not the same *person* as the one he addressed as "Father"—and who identified Jesus as "beloved Son" (Mark 1:11; 9:7).

Jesus knew that he was divine, and he applied unmistakably divine titles to himself, such as "lord of the sabbath" (Luke 6:5). His appeal to God as "Father" was perceived as a divine claim, which the Pharisees condemned as blasphemy and supreme arrogance. "This was why the Jews sought all the more to kill him, because he ... called God his Father, making himself equal with God" (John 5:18). And Jesus did not back away from those charges. Instead, he expressed his expectation "that all may honor the Son, even as they honor the Father" (John 5:23).

From the reactions of his opponents, we can see that Jesus' self-understanding was scandalous. Nevertheless, the disciples and evangelists reported the Master's divine titles and claims without commentary, explanation, or defense. They had received a *revelation*—an idea usually rendered by the Greek *apokalypsis*, which means "unveiling." Jesus had shown them something that had previously been veiled from human sight, something humanity could not have discovered on its own. The Apsotles were duty-bound to report the content of the revelation, even though they could not pretend to comprehend it.

Jesus had, moreover, spoken of a third divine Person—distinct from the Father and Son yet united to them. Jesus spoke of the Holy Spirit as someone like himself: "another Counselor" (John 14:16)—yet, again, someone whom the Father could "give" and "send" (John 14:26). The Holy Spirit would himself be an active agent—a person and not a force—teaching and reminding the disciples of all that they needed to know.

The divinity of the Spirit was self-evident to the Apostles. In his interrogation of the wayward Ananias and Sapphira, Peter used the terms *God* and *Holy Spirit* interchangeably (compare Acts 5:4 and 5:9).

Such was the God proclaimed by the Apostles—and experienced by thousands of people in the New Testament period.

* * *

Christians, over time, would reflect on the mystery and see hints of it in the Old Testament. They noticed that the creation story portrays God using the first person plural, *us* and *our*, to speak of himself and not the singular *me* and *my*: "Let us make man in *our* image, after *our* likeness" (Gen. 1:26, emphasis added). God is one, and his singularity is reflected in the verb forms of the narrative; and yet, when he speaks, he speaks as a collective.

Later in the book of Genesis, God's promise appears to Abraham by means of three messengers. Other books of the Bible present God's wisdom as a person (see Proverbs 1:20 and chapters 7–9). Similarly, "the word of the Lord" appears often as not simply a *message*, but a *messenger*, who comes and goes (for example, 1 Kings 17:2). When Jews in the diaspora composed the *Targums*, paraphrased and expanded versions of the books of the Bible, they often depicted "the Word" (Aramaic *memra*) as a personal figure.

The most prominent Jewish contemporary of the Apostles, Philo of Alexandria, speculated much about God's "Word." Philo personifies the Word as the mediator of God's revelation; God is known in and through the Word. For Philo, the Word is a *deuteros theos*—a "second god"!—and yet is also the archetype of man.[19]

Other religious Jews were discussing the possibility of a plurality of "powers" in heaven.[20] Yet none went so far as the author of the fourth Gospel, who wrote: "In the beginning was the Word, and the Word was with God, and the Word was God.... And the Word became flesh and dwelt among us" (John 1:1, 14). For the early Christians the Word was eternal and transcendent, but became a man in order to save the human race. The apostolic Faith proclaimed the eternal "Word" as enfleshed in the historical Jesus.

The word *flesh* (Greek *sarx*) was graphic and must have been scandalous. The same term could be used to describe meat hanging in the marketplace. Here it describes the human body of God. (Later, in John 6:51, Jesus will use the same term, *sarx*, to describe his body given as "bread ... for the life of the world.")

---

[19] For a discussion of Philo's doctrine of the Word, see David T. Runia, *Philo in Early Christian Literature: A Survey* (Minneapolis: Fortress Press, 1993), 79–83. See also Alan F. Segal, *Rebecca's Children: Judaism and Christianity in the Roman World* (Cambridge: Harvard University Press, 1986), 154–155.

[20] For a study of the relevant literature, see Alan F. Segal, *Two Powers in Heaven: Early Rabbinic Reports about Christianity and Gnosticism* (Boston: Brill, 2002).

The New Testament doctrine of God was revealed at Pentecost—revealed in the words of St. Peter and in the event itself. But nowhere in Scripture is it presented systematically. The word *Trinity* appears nowhere in the Bible.

Nevertheless, the testimony of the Apostles is clear. The awaited Messiah, sent by God, was not merely one of the great men of history, but rather God himself. The Holy Spirit, promised by Jesus, in turn, was not an impersonal gift, but the gift of a divine person. From the beginning, the Church instinctively worshipped Jesus and the Holy Spirit as God. St. Paul prayed to the Father and Jesus together:

> Now may our God and Father himself, and our Lord Jesus, direct our way to you; and may the Lord make you increase and abound in love to one another and to all men, as we do to you, so that he may establish your hearts unblamable in holiness before our God and Father, at the coming of our Lord Jesus with all his saints. (1 Thess. 3:11–13)

Paul also pronounced blessings in Jesus' name (Rom. 16:20; 1 Cor. 16:23) and in the name of the Trinity: "The grace of the Lord Jesus Christ and the love of God and the fellowship of the Holy Spirit be with you all" (2 Cor. 13:14).

The most ancient Christian homily we possess outside Scripture begins with the line: "Brethren, it is fitting that you should think of Jesus Christ as of God, as the Judge of the living and the dead."[21] And one of the earliest *pagan* reports about Christianity, the letter of Pliny the Younger to the emperor Trajan, describes a congregation gathered to "sing

---

[21] The pseudonymous *Second Epistle of Clement.*

hymns to Christ as to a god."[22] The New Testament contains several passages that testify to Jesus' divinity and that seem to be cast in a musical form (John 1:1–18; Phil. 2:5–11; Col. 1:11–15). Hymns to the divine Christ were likely part of Christian worship from the beginning.

What was implicit in Scripture became explicit in the Church's worship—and made more explicit still in the speculative theology of the following generations. By the end of the second century, Greek and Latin writers had coined new words to describe the mystery of the three in one: *Trinas* in Greek, *Trinitas* in Latin[23]—the etymological sources of the English word *Trinity*.[24]

But the earliest proof is in the Church's worship of God as Father, and of Jesus, and of the Holy Spirit. A maxim of the early Church tells us: The law of prayer is the law of belief.[25] And the Church has prayed consistently in a Trinitarian way since the time of the Apostles.

* * *

The God revealed at Pentecost was not a new God. He was, as the disciples proclaimed to the Jews in Jerusalem, "the God

---

[22] Pliny the Younger was the Roman governor of Bithynia, around A.D. 112. His report on Christianity takes place in his correspondence with the emperor Trajan, *Epistulae* 10.96.

[23] See Theophilus of Antioch, *Apologia ad Autolycum* 2.15; Tertullian, *Adversus Praxeam* 25.

[24] The best and most accessible introduction to the doctrine of the Trinity and its dramatic development through the early centuries of the Church is James L. Papandrea, *Trinity 101: Father, Son, Holy Spirit* (Liguori, MO: Liguori Publications, 2012).

[25] See Prosper of Aquitaine, quoted in the *Catechism of the Catholic Church*, no. 1124.

of Abraham and of Isaac and of Jacob, the God of our fathers" (Acts 3:13; 7:32).

The *experience* of that God was decidedly different. The eternal Word had "pitched his tent" among his people; that's the literal meaning of the Greek in John 1:14. And, as if that were not close enough, he promised that they would share his life in a still deeper way. He would "abide" in them, and they would abide in him (John 15:4–10). They would be "filled" with the Holy Spirit (Acts 2:4; 4:8; 6:3, 5; 7:55; 13:52).

God would live in the believers, as believers lived in God. God shared human nature, so that humans might come to share his divine nature. St. Paul said: "For you know the grace of our Lord Jesus Christ, that though he was rich, yet for your sake he became poor, so that by his poverty you might become rich" (2 Cor. 8:9; see also Gal. 4:4–6). As Jesus was the Son of God, so the members of his Body, the Church, would know themselves to be children of God (see 1 John 3:1–2).

This was the deepest meaning of salvation. Jesus came "to save his people from their sins" (Matt. 1:21); but the cleansing from sin was a preparation for their new life *as God's children.* Around the same time the Fathers were developing a language to describe the Trinity, they were coining terms just as bold to describe salvation. They called it *divinization* and *deification,* to emphasize the reality that Christians were God's children. Jesus' promise of the Spirit was not a word game. It was the promise of a share in God's very nature (see 2 Pet. 1:4).[26]

[26]An outstanding study of this doctrine is Daniel A. Keating, *Deification and Grace* (Naples, FL: Sapientia Press, 2007). See also Michael J. Christensen and Jeffery A. Wittung, eds., *Partakers of the Divine Nature: The History and Development of Deification in the Christian Tradition* (Grand Rapids, MI: Baker, 2007).

That sudden infusion of divine power explains the ecstatic behavior of the disciples on the day of Pentecost. It also explains the power with which the Apostles worked miracles from that day forward. It is perhaps the only plausible explanation for the success of the work of evangelization in those first generations. The sociologist Rodney Stark estimates that the Christian Church grew, over its first three centuries, at a steady rate of 40 percent per decade.[27]

That's not something the Apostles—as we know them from the New Testament—could accomplish. Remember: Peter was a coward, Thomas a doubter, James and John ambitious dreamers.

With military might and a wealth of resources, Alexander the Great had failed to conquer the world. So had imperial Rome. Yet believers, or rather Christ, who lived in them (Gal. 2:20) and enabled them to act with his divine power, would succeed.

---

[27] Rodney Stark, *The Rise of Christianity* (San Francisco: Harper-Collins, 1997).

CHAPTER 5
Disturbing the Priests

Most of the names we know from ancient times, we know not from literature but from monuments. Parchment and papyrus can rot away in a generation's time. An inscription in granite can still look crisp after millennia.

These were the people (usually men) who inspired respect or fear. Their names were chiseled in stone, at great expense, by skilled labor.

Some of the names we find in the New Testament have also been unearthed on stone—King Herod, for example, and the Roman emperors Augustus and Tiberius. Most of the characters at the center of the drama, however, were less famous while they lived. Although the Apostles later came to rank among the most important figures in history, during their lifetime they went mostly unnoticed. They were certainly not the sort of people who lived to see their names carved in stone.

But some of their adversaries were. The name of the Roman prefect Pontius Pilate turned up, not long ago, on a dedicatory stone from a building he constructed in honor of the emperor Tiberius.

Far more *personal* an inscription, however, was found on the ossuary—the bone box, or casket—that contained the mortal remains of Joseph Caiaphas, the high priest who led the plot to bring about Jesus' trial and execution. The casket is richly decorated, ornately carved with floral and geometric patterns. Twice the name *Yehosef bar Kayafa*—Joseph, son of Caiaphas—appears on its sides. It was found among other beautiful ossuaries carefully laid in a cave that served as his family's tomb.[28]

Both Pontius Pilate and Joseph Caiaphas were important men, respected and feared. They were the kind of men who live to supervise the construction of their own monuments.

Both were accomplished men who had risen far in their chosen fields. As Roman prefect and as chief priest of the Jews, Pilate and Caiaphas had to deal often with one another, negotiating a fragile peace and maintaining a difficult order in the land it was their lot to share.

[28] For an interesting study of Caiaphas in archaeology, see Rick Guy, "Head and Corner Stone," in *The Priest*, April 2012, archived at osv.com.

Each man seems to have had a measure of respect for the other and his people—oddly mixed with a measure of contempt.

* * *

Priesthood is by definition a sacrificial office. A priest is a mediator between God and mankind; he offers sacrifice to God on behalf of his people. "For every high priest chosen from among men is appointed to act on behalf of men in relation to God, to offer gifts and sacrifices for sins" (Heb. 5:1).

The role bore a degree of prestige, because Israel's religion centered on sacrifice, which could take place only in Jerusalem's Temple and could be offered only by a priest.

Priesthood was reserved by law to the tribe of Levi, and its hierarchy had three tiers. The priests and their assistants, called Levites, carried out the ordinary, everyday, prescribed ritual offerings in the Temple. Members of the tribe of Levi rotated their periods of ministry. Although their homes were in various places, during their term of service they took up residence in or near Jerusalem, and there they observed strict celibacy for their entire period of ministry.[29]

At the top of the hierarchy was the high priest. He held the most important ceremonial office, presiding at the Jerusalem Temple. Only he could enter the Temple's Holy of Holies, and he could do so only once a year, to offer sacrifice on the Day of Atonement, Yom Kippur. The law dictated that the high

[29]Brant Pitre, "Jesus, the New Temple, and the New Priesthood," in Scott W. Hahn and David Scott, eds., *Letter and Spirit*, vol. 4 (Steubenville, OH: Saint Paul Center for Biblical Theology, 2004), 76.

priest, once ordained, should hold the office for the remainder of his life.

But during the dynasty of the Herods—and even their predecessors—the office of high priesthood had become a reward for political loyalty. King Herod the Great, who reigned when Jesus was born, installed and removed high priests at will, and some he murdered. By the time of Jesus' adulthood, the office went exclusively to candidates whom the ruling powers considered to be reliable.

For much of the first century, the high priesthood was occupied by various members of the family of a priest named Ananus (shortened as Annas in the New Testament; see Luke 3:2). They adapted the rules for the sake of political expedience. Rather than hold the office for life, they kept it till they lost interest or lost favor with the rulers. Annas lived to see the brief high-priestly terms of several offspring and in-laws; and many people believed he remained the real power behind the altar. The Gospels may bear subtle, wry commentary on this situation. Luke speaks of the rule of Caiaphas, Annas's son-in-law, as "the high-priesthood of Annas and Caiaphas" (Luke 3:2), as if it had been shared by equals. Although the term of the office was the life of the occupant, John observes at one point that Caiaphas "was high priest *that year*" (John 18:13, emphasis added).

A high priest should have been honored, and should have wielded influence, but many religious Jews now viewed the high priest with contempt. The Essenes believed the office had been so corrupted as to become illegitimate. They rejected its occupants, the Temple service, and even the calendar of feasts observed in Jerusalem. They awaited the Messiah who would restore the sacral order in its purity.

The degradation of the priesthood served also to enhance the popularity of the Pharisees, who observed strict discipline and were averse to compromise in religious matters.

Jesus, for his part, found it necessary to "cleanse" the Temple (John 2:14–21), driving out the merchants who sold animals for sacrifice and exchanged foreign money for the coin of Jerusalem. He made the seemingly outlandish claim that, if the Temple were destroyed, he would rebuild it in three days. These words would be cited against him during his trial, as evidence of sedition (see Matt. 26:61; 27:40).

* * *

By the time of Jesus' trial, the rule of the Herods had been divided among several heirs approved by Rome; and these kings were, unlike their despotic ancestor, mostly figureheads. Upon Herod the Great's death, many people made it clear that they would prefer a Roman governor to a local tyrant (whose claim to Jewishness was derided).

The Romans were pleased to comply with the request. They established a large military presence in the land, and they assigned a prefect to the region. The fifth man to hold that office was Pontius Pilate, who governed from the years 26 to 36.

Pilate could be brutal. He showed little sensitivity to Jewish customs, and it was he who made the fateful decision to move the Roman army from its pagan outpost to Jerusalem. With the army came images—on shields and banners—of Caesar and of the Roman gods. The very presence of such idols was considered pollution. Pilate had profaned the holy city. Pious Jews protested, but Pilate refused to budge, as any concession could be perceived as an insult to Caesar.

Pilate also seized money from the Temple treasury to fund important public works.[30]

Although the Temple officials raised protests at all the appropriate moments, they did not present a serious threat to Pilate or to Rome. History and Herod had schooled the priests in the art of compromise. They had the support of the aristocratic landholders and merchants—and the religious Sadducees. They knew how to protect the upper class's common interests through shrewd cooperation.

* * *

Jesus' talk about the Temple seemed threatening to Jerusalem's priests. Perhaps they had good reasons to be nervous about the security of their social status. The Pharisees opposed the priestly Sadducees on doctrinal grounds, and the Essenes judged the Jerusalem clergy to be phonies. Among the documents found in the Essenes' library at Qumran was a manual for waging war, fighting alongside angels, to restore the proper religious order in Jerusalem.

Annas, Caiaphas, and their family probably saw themselves —with their diplomatic prudence and political savvy—as Jerusalem's only hope for survival.

Herod had removed and even massacred priests. What was to keep Rome from doing the same if the place began to appear unstable? And then what would happen to Jerusalem?

The number of disciples steadily grew as the Apostles preached openly in the vicinity of the Temple. The Apostles possessed an authority—and won a respect—that the old

---

[30]Pilate's offenses against the Jews are detailed in Josephus, *Antiquities of the Jews* 18.3–4.

guard could not force or coerce. When a man tried to deceive Simon Peter, the Apostle responded: "You have not lied to men but to God" (Acts 5:4). He was claiming, implicitly, to be God's vicar, his *mediator*, and thus his priest—and yet Peter had neither the ancestry nor the training for such an office.

Jesus himself had performed priestly acts, although he was not a Levite. At the Last Supper, he offered his own Body and Blood as a memorial sacrifice. What gave him the right to act as a priest? In the letter to the Hebrews, we find a first-generation author arguing that Jesus' priesthood came not from the tribe of Levi, but from the more ancient "order of Melchizedek" (Hebrews 5–7). The priesthood of Levi originated during the Exodus (see Numbers 18); but Melchizedek's priesthood existed long before that, as attested in Gen. 14:18–20. Melchizedek is the first figure the Bible refers to as a priest. He was, moreover, a king; and so, in time, King Solomon—although not a Levite—claimed to possess a royal priesthood in "the line of Melchizedek" (Ps. 110:4).

More and more, as the Church grew, the Apostles came to speak of their work in priestly and sacrificial terms. St. Paul wrote to the Romans:

> But on some points I have written to you very boldly by way of reminder, because of the grace given me by God to be a minister of Christ Jesus to the Gentiles in the priestly service of the gospel of God, so that the offering of the Gentiles may be acceptable, sanctified by the Holy Spirit. (Rom. 15:15–16)

The English does not make it as clear as it would be to Paul's original readers. The word *minister* is a translation of *leitourgon*, a term that emphasizes the priest's role in ritual worship (liturgy). *Hierourgounta* is well rendered as "priestly service," a term used for the work of the priests in the Jerusalem Temple. *Offering* (*prosphora*) is a term typically applied to sacrificial victims. Other words in the passage have similar connotations.

Elsewhere, Paul compared himself to the priests in Jerusalem, insisting that he had the same rights as they (1 Cor. 9:13). He also described himself and his fellow Apostles, again in priestly terms, as "stewards of the mysteries of God" (1 Cor. 4:1)—"mysteries" (Greek *mysterion*) being the liturgical rites conducted by a priest.

To the ears of the high-priestly family, this language would sound subversive. It seemed to subvert not only the sacred order, but also the civic order, because the priests in Jerusalem were mediators not only between God and the Chosen People, but also between the Chosen People and their earthly rulers, the Romans. They had confidence in their own ability to mediate that latter relationship. They had kept a lid on religious rebellion for a full generation. They had no such confidence in the qualifications of the Apostles.

The Apostles could be seen only as a danger, a threat, to the priests—and so to the Roman prefect, too.

CHAPTER 6
The Crown of Martyrdom

Jesus' opponents felt sure that his execution would solve the problem that he had become. That was the way Roman authority typically dealt with troublesome religious movements—with exemplary public violence. Once the charismatic leaders were removed and the treasuries emptied, the followers usually lost their ardor for the cause.

Crucifixion was a particularly gruesome, humiliating, and torturous death. It was the cruelest method of executions the Romans had devised; and they reserved it for the worst crimes committed by men considered to be lowlife criminals. In most cases, it quashed movements instantly. Jesus himself made note of the principle at work: "strike the shepherd, and the sheep will be scattered" (Mark 14:27).

But Jesus' execution solved nothing for the Romans, for the Jerusalem priests, or for the Pharisees. Quite the contrary: it made matters worse. As reports of the Master's empty tomb went abroad, his popularity took an upturn, and so the conflict continued and grew, now with ever more numerous disciples taking the place of Jesus in the struggle with the Jerusalem authorities.

Opposition, it seems, was an unavoidable part of the life of the disciples. Jesus himself said: "I will send ... apostles, some of whom they will kill and persecute" (Luke 11:49). In another account, he made it clear that such opposition would be universal, marked by Roman crucifixions and Jewish scourging (Matt. 23:34). He assured his disciples that, contrary to all appearances, persecution would be the occasion of great blessings:

> Blessed are those who are persecuted for righteousness' sake, for theirs is the kingdom of heaven. Blessed are you when men revile you and persecute you and utter all kinds of evil against you falsely on my account. Rejoice and be glad, for your reward is great in heaven, for so men persecuted the prophets who were before you. (Matt. 5:10–12)

In the same sermon, Jesus instructed his hearers: "Love your enemies and pray for those who persecute you" (Matt. 5:44) —which is counterintuitive advice, to say the least.

Persecution was a recurring theme in Jesus' preaching. He made clear that it was inevitable (Luke 21:12) but that it should not be sought. Persecution should be avoided if possible (Matt. 10:23). It would be the occasion for some to lose their faith (Mark 4:17). Those who persevered, however, would be rewarded—so greatly that they would come to see persecution itself as a reward (Mark 10:30).

The Apostles, in turn, experienced persecution and came to expect it: "Indeed all who desire to live a godly life in Christ Jesus will be persecuted" (2 Tim. 3:12). Occasionally it would come in waves over the entire Church, as it did in Jerusalem (Acts 8:1), in Pisidian Antioch (Acts 13:50), in Iconium and Lystra (2 Tim. 3:11), and elsewhere.

The early Christians came to apply the word *persecution* to any obstacles to the fulfillment of their mission. If the obstacles were not willed directly by men, they were seen as persecutions of the devil (Rev. 2:10). Calamities, famines, peril, and hardships would try believers and test their faith, but they did not themselves have the power to "separate" a Christian "from the love of Christ" (Rom. 8:35). When Christians were weak, then, paradoxically, they were strong (2 Cor. 12:10).

The authorities in Jerusalem expected public flogging and executions to induce terror and shame. For the disciples of Jesus, however, persecution in every form became a blessing—and even a reason for boasting (see 2 Thess. 1:4). When Paul "boasts" of his accomplishments to the Corinthians, one thing he makes sure to mention is that he was flogged in public five times (2 Cor. 11:24). Persecution was, for the Church, a sign of success, a mark of resemblance to Jesus, who had said: "'A servant is not greater than his master.' If they persecuted me, they will persecute you" (John 15:20).

* * *

It should come as no surprise, then, that St. Luke dedicates so much narrative, in the Acts of the Apostles, to the story of the first disciple to be persecuted unto death.

His name was Stephen. He was "full of faith," "full of grace and power," "full of ... the Holy Spirit" (Acts 6:5, 8). Steeped in the history of Israel, he was eloquent and persuasive. Admired even by the Apostles, he was chosen among the first deacons to assist them in the administration of the Church. The book of Acts has only twenty-eight chapters, and two of them are devoted almost entirely to the works and words of Stephen.

Because he was persecuted unto death, Stephen's story loomed large—for centuries to come—in the imagination and conversation of Christians. The Church would have almost universal outlaw status, for more than 250 years, from the age of the Apostles until the reign of Constantine. Persecution was indeed, as Jesus and the Apostles had predicted, the normal condition of Christian life.

Stephen's story provided Christians a framework for the understanding of all subsequent persecutions. Luke's narrative, in fact, presents Stephen's trial and death as strikingly similar to those of Jesus.

With "great wonders and signs among the people," Stephen aroused the envy and fear of synagogue leaders and the Temple priests. They conspired against him. They fabricated charges against him—the same charges that had been leveled against Jesus: that he had spoken against the Temple and blasphemed "against Moses and God." The authorities brought him to trial, interrogated him, and condemned him. His death was the occasion for a confession of Jesus as the Son of God. While dying, he asked God not to hold the sin of murder against his killers. And he asked Jesus to receive his spirit.

In every detail, Stephen's life and death are presented as a faithful imitation of the Passion of Jesus. Much later in the book, one of the Apostles would apply a term to Stephen that has become the Church's technical term for a Christian persecuted unto death. Stephen is called God's *martyros* (Acts 22:20). To Greek speakers of the first century, the word meant simply "witness"—a witness in a court of law—someone who gave *testimony*, the word for which was *martyrion*.

The New Testament speaks often of witness. Jesus told the Apostles that they would be his witnesses to the ends of the earth, and they described themselves as witnesses of his Resurrection.

Witness can be active or passive. In English we use the same word to describe someone who sees something (an eyewitness) and someone who testifies to it. In Greek, such passive eyewitnesses are described by the word *autoptai* (as in Luke 1:2). Jesus, however, expected the Apostles not simply to *see* the events of salvation, but to *testify* to them—to give public testimony through their words and deeds.

Stephen is called a witness, and the term became so closely associated with him—and with the act of dying for Christ —that the original meanings of *martus* and *martyrion* were soon eclipsed. A third-century Scripture scholar from Egypt, Origen of Alexandria, explained how the word *martyr* acquired its Christian definition.

> Now everyone who bears witness to the truth, whether he support it by words or deeds, or in whatever way, may properly be called a witness (*martyr*). But it has become the custom of the brotherhood, since they are struck with admiration of those who have contended to the death for truth and valor, to keep the name of *martyr* more properly for those who have borne witness

to the mystery of godliness by shedding their blood for it.[31]

Stephen's name—in Greek, *Stephanos*—means "crown." As Stephen was honored in the Church as the *protomartyr*, or first martyr, the early Christians often punned on his name, saying that those who died for the faith would receive a "martyr's crown." This may be the case even in the book of Revelation, where the Lord tells the Church of Ephesus: "Be faithful unto death, and I will give you the crown [*stephanon*] of life" (Rev. 2:10). The murals in the Roman catacombs and other works of early Christian art typically depict the martyrs wearing or holding crowns, the universal sign of membership in the order of St. Stephen—the order of martyrs.

* * *

As Jesus' death was a once-for-all sacrifice, so the Church saw the death of the martyrs in similarly sacrificial terms. In the book of Revelation, John sees "under the altar the souls of those who had been slain for the word of God and for the witness [*martyrian*] they had borne" (Rev. 6:9). The word he uses for altar means "place of sacrifice." The martyrs are those who most perfectly carry out the exhortation of the Apostle Paul: "I appeal to you therefore, brethren, by the mercies of God, to *present your bodies as a living sacrifice*, holy and acceptable to God, which is *your spiritual worship*" (Rom. 12:1, emphasis added).

The early Christians consistently presented martyrdom in liturgical terms.[32] They looked at it as the most perfect

---

[31] Origen, *Commentary on John* 2.28.
[32] On the relationship between martyrdom and Eucharist, see Robin Darling Young, *In Procession Before the World: Martyrdom*

imitation of the Eucharistic Christ. As Jesus laid down his life (John 15:13), he made an offering of his Body and Blood under the appearance of bread and wine (Luke 22:19–20). Jesus identified himself with those elements (John 6:51–56). So did the martyrs, in their turn. St. Paul foresaw that he would "be poured as a libation," a "sacrificial offering" (Phil. 2:17; see also 2 Tim. 4:6).

Many in the generation immediately following the Apostles were pleased to associate their death with the action of Christ in the Sacrifice of the Altar. In A.D. 107, St. Ignatius of Antioch, as he made his journey to be executed in Rome, wrote: "I am God's wheat. Let me be ground by the teeth of the wild beasts, that I may become the pure bread of Christ."[33] His greatest wish, he said, was to be "a libation to God while the altar is still ready."[34] He spoke of the Roman Church as a choir, "singing together" at his offering in the arena. He quoted the ancient Eucharistic prayers as he said he had come "from East to West" so that such an offering could be made.

---

as *Public Liturgy in Early Christianity* (Milwaukee: Marquette University Press, 2001); Finbarr G. Clancy, S.J., "Imitating the Mysteries That You Celebrate: Martyrdom and Eucharist in the Early Patristic Period," in *The Great Persecution: The Proceedings of the Fifth Patristic Conference*, Maynooth, 2003 (Dublin: Four Courts, 2009), 106–140; Joseph Cardinal Ratzinger, *Pilgrim Fellowship of Faith: The Church as Communion* (San Francisco: Ignatius, 2005), 112–114; George Heyman, *The Power of Sacrifice: Roman and Christian Discourses in Conflict* (Washington, DC: Catholic University of America Press, 2007), 184–185. See also Pope Benedict XVI, Post-Synodal Apostolic Exhortation *Sacramentum Caritatis*, no. 85.

[33] St. Ignatius of Antioch, *Letter to the Romans* 4.
[34] Ibid., 2.

Ignatius's contemporary and correspondent, Polycarp of Smyrna, also died as a martyr. A disciple of the Apostle John, Polycarp was made a bishop while a young man and served effectively for many years before his trial and execution. The account of his death is the earliest description of a martyrdom we have, apart from Scripture. Set down by an eyewitness, Polycarp's secretary, the text presents the bishop's last words as a long prayer that follows the structure of the Eucharistic prayers—thanksgiving, petition, praise, and doxology—and echoes their language.

At the end he prays:

> May I be accepted this day before you as a rich and acceptable sacrifice, as you, the ever-truthful God, have prepared and have revealed beforehand to me, and now have fulfilled. So, too, I praise you for all things, I bless you, I glorify you, along with the everlasting and heavenly Jesus Christ, your beloved Son. With him, to you and the Holy Spirit, be glory both now and to all coming ages. Amen.[35]

As flames closed in on the body of Polycarp (the eyewitness tells us), the onlookers smelled not the stench of burning flesh, but rather the aroma of baking bread and incense, two elements typically associated with the Christian liturgy.[36]

* * *

Martyrdom was indeed a vivid and compelling witness to the communion of life Christ shared with his disciples. "But

[35] *Martyrdom of Polycarp* 14.
[36] Ibid., 15.

if we have died with Christ," Paul said, "we believe that we shall also live with him" (Rom. 6:8). Christians could be God's children only if they were willing to share the suffering of the only-begotten Son—"we are ... heirs with Christ, provided we suffer with him in order that we may also be glorified with him" (Rom. 8:16–17).

Martyrdom, then, was not some extreme form of masochism. Nor was it a method of suicide. It was laying down one's life in imitation of Jesus. It was giving one's entire life in loving sacrifice, as Jesus did. Christians believed it was well worth the reward. St. Paul had written: "I consider that the sufferings of this present time are not worth comparing with the glory that is to be revealed to us" (Rom. 8:18). Given those terms, martyrdom was, in the words of one modern sociologist, a "rational choice":[37] "while membership [in the Church] was expensive, it was, in fact, a bargain."[38]

Many, apparently, made that choice. Persecutions raged intermittently until A.D. 313, when Christianity was legalized by the emperor Constantine's Edict of Milan. We do not know how many died as martyrs. Scholars differ in their estimates, but the numbers were surely in the thousands—and perhaps hundreds of thousands. The documentary evidence, from both pagan and Christian witnesses, is extensive.[39]

According to ancient tradition, all the Apostles suffered publicly for the Faith, and most died as martyrs. Yet even the

[37] Rodney Stark, *The Rise of Christianity* (San Francisco: Harper, 1997), 165.
[38] Ibid., 188.
[39] See W.H.C. Frend, *Martyrdom and Persecution in the Early Church: A Study of a Conflict from the Maccabees to Donatus* (Grand Rapids, MI: Baker, 1965).

Christians who died in their beds had the opportunity to give witness. The biblical scholar Origen testified to the universality of the vocation to *martyrion*—to Christian witness.

> The Savior gives the name of *martyr* to every one who bears witness to the truth he declares. At the Ascension he says to his disciples: "you shall be my witnesses in Jerusalem and in all Judea and Samaria and to the end of the earth" (Acts 1:8). The leper who was cleansed (Matthew 8:4) had still to bring the gift that Moses commanded for a testimony to those who did not believe in the Christ. In the same way the martyrs bear witness for a testimony to the unbelieving, and so do all the saints whose deeds shine before men. They spend their life rejoicing in the cross of Christ and bearing witness to the true light.[40]

Martyrdom made a powerful impression on the pagans who witnessed it. The first-century philosopher Epictetus expressed his grudging admiration, as did the second-century emperor Marcus Aurelius and his contemporary, the physician Galen.

Many, like the second-century philosopher Justin of Samaria, saw the Christians' testimony of blood and believed. At the end of that century, an African lawyer named Tertullian, also a convert to the Faith, taunted his persecutors: "As often as we are mown down by you, the more we grow in numbers; the blood of the Christians is seed."[41]

[40]Origen, *Commentary on John* 2.28.
[41]Tertullian, *Apology* 50.13.

The fact should never arrive as news. It is as old as the Gospel:

> Truly, truly, I say to you, unless a grain of wheat falls into the earth and dies, it remains alone; but if it dies, it bears much fruit. (John 12:24)

CHAPTER 7

Saul the Persecutor, Paul the Apostle

Stephen died at the hands of a mob—men who were "enraged" (Acts 7:54) by his accusations. His murderers were many, but we know the name of just one of them: Saul.[42] St. Luke tells us: "Saul was consenting

---

[42] In this chapter, I wish to acknowledge my debt, not to a book, but to a friendship. Much of what I know of Saul of Tarsus I learned in conversation with my longtime colleague Scott Hahn. I worked with him to establish the Saint Paul Center for Biblical Theology and have been associated with that institution, in one way or another, since its founding in 2001. Hahn's two books that discuss Saul/Paul in greatest detail are *Kinship by Covenant: A Canonical Approach to the Fulfillment of God's Saving Promises* (New Haven, CT: Yale, Anchor Bible Reference Library, 2009) and *A Pocket Guide to Saint Paul* (Huntington, IN: Our Sunday Visitor, 2008).

to his death" (Acts 8:1). Members of the mob left their cloaks with him as they took up stones to kill Stephen (Acts 7:58).

That day marked the beginning of the first coordinated, systematic persecution of the Church. Most of the disciples fled Jerusalem and went into hiding. Some took refuge among Israel's most notorious apostates, in Samaria, where the Pharisees and other religious authorities would be unlikely to venture. Only the Apostles stayed behind in the holy city.

Saul, a young Pharisee consumed by zeal, pursued a program to purge Jerusalem—and every Jewish community—of any trace of Jesus' teaching or influence. Single-minded in his dedication to the task, he went about "breathing threats and murder against the disciples of the Lord" (Acts 9:1). "But Saul laid waste the church, and entering house after house, he dragged off men and women and committed them to prison" (Acts 8:3).

Saul was not a docile minion, blindly carrying out orders issued by higher authorities. He was the most active agent of persecution, moving it forward and prosecuting the matter himself. Not content with a local police action, he "went to the high priest and asked him for letters to the synagogues at Damascus, so that if he found any belonging to the Way, men or women, he might bring them bound to Jerusalem" (Acts 9:1–2). He was willing to travel 140 miles, from Jerusalem to Damascus, by foot or by horse, to round up disciples of Jesus and bring them to the same end as Stephen. The mere mention of Saul's name was enough to strike fear in the heart of those who followed Jesus' way (see Acts 9:13–14).

Among the Church's persecutors, Saul was singular in his zeal, unabashed in his purpose. He saw no reason to be diplomatic or cautious about it. He was willing to take risks, even if he was perceived to be a radical. Saul was a man with a mission.

* * *

From his earliest days, Saul had sense of divine calling. His birthplace, Tarsus, was a bustling coastal city and administrative center for the Roman province of Cilicia (what is now southeastern Turkey). Like his father, Saul was a tradesman—a tentmaker. Like his father, he held Roman citizenship, a coveted privilege. Like his father, he observed the doctrine and discipline of the Pharisees.

He grew up with a strong sense that God had set him aside for a special task. His calling came even before his birth—*koilias metros mou*, as he put it, "from my mother's womb." While still a youth, he "advanced in Judaism," he said, "beyond many of my own age among my people, so extremely zealous was I for the traditions of my fathers" (Gal. 1:14–15).

A prodigy, he went early to Jerusalem to study in the great center of Jewish learning. At the time, there were two rival schools in the city, following two first-century sages who took two different—and sometimes opposing—approaches to the law. They were the school of Hillel and the school of Shammai. They flourished around the time of Jesus' birth. It is said that the two sages debated and differed on more than three hundred important points of law, liturgy, morality, and theology. Shammai tended to be strict and exclusive in his interpretation. Hillel tended to be lenient. An ancient maxim (preserved by the House of Hillel) runs: "Be gentle like Hillel and not impatient like Shammai."[43]

By the time Saul arrived in Jerusalem, both men were dead. The young man—perhaps still a boy—took up study

---

[43] Quoted in Jacob Neusner, *Judaism in the Beginning of Christianity* (Minneapolis, MN: Fortress, 1984), 84.

under Hillel's grandson and successor, Gamaliel, who would be known to Jews ever after as Gamaliel the Great, and *Rabban*, which means "Our Master." He is one of the sages most often cited in the Mishnah and the Babylonian Talmud. The Mishnah looks back to Gamaliel's lifetime as a kind of Golden Age: "Since Rabban Gamaliel the Elder died, there has been no more reverence for the law, and purity and piety died out at the same time."[44]

Gamaliel appears once in the Acts of the Apostles (5:34-39), where he exemplifies the ideals associated with his school. As a member of the Sanhedrin, he pleads lenience and tolerance for the Apostles.

Saul would later boast that he had studied under the greatest rabbi in the House of Hillel. But historians and other observers have long noted that Saul's sympathies seemed to lie more with the House of Shammai.

If Shammai was impatient, as the maxim taught, it was because of his zeal for the law and his eagerness to bring about the day of the Messiah. Some teachers believed that faithful observance of the Torah was the precondition of God's saving action. Through the prophets, God had promised salvation and vindication to Israel—a gathering of the tribes, a restoration of the land, and an expulsion or subjugation of the foreign powers. The New Testament scholar N.T. Wright summarizes the situation:

> The Shammaites, and the revolutionaries in general, were eager to bring these prophecies to fulfillment by their zeal for the Torah. They would not sit around and

---

[44]*Mishnah Sotah* 15:18.

wait; they would take matters into their own hands....
Observing Torah would hasten the time of fulfillment.
If God were to act climactically now, within history,
while Israel was still not keeping Torah properly, she
would be condemned along with the Gentiles.[45]

It seems likely that Saul fell under the influence of ideas
like these. He saw the disciples of Jesus as heretics who opposed observance of the law and denied the holiness of the
Temple. Jesus, after all, had repeatedly violated the laws regarding the Sabbath—healing people, encouraging his disciples to pick grain, and so on. He even declared himself to be
"Lord of the Sabbath," thus putting himself in the place of God.

Saul believed that such heretics should be given a choice.
They should adopt a strict observance of the law—or they
should die, so that they would not bring divine judgment
down on the rest of the nation. They were an obstacle to the
fulfillment of the prophecies and the coming of the Christ.
They were an impediment to the destiny of Israel.

* * *

The blood of the martyrs, as we saw in the last chapter, is the
seed of the Church.

The disciples who fled Jerusalem were hardly cowed into
silence. St. Luke reports that "those who were scattered went
about preaching the word" (Acts 8:4). This new persecution,
like the death of Jesus before it, just exacerbated the problem
for the Jerusalem authorities.

---

[45] N.T. Wright, *What Saint Paul Really Said* (Grand Rapids, MI:
Eerdmans, 1997), 31.

Wherever the disciples fled, they made new disciples, as the subsequent chapters of the Acts of the Apostles make clear. They fled to Antioch, and in that city they were, for the first time, called Christians (Acts 11:26). This new nickname—which may have been derogatory—did not indicate a new religion, different from that of Israel. Not even Saul considered Jesus' disciples to be Gentiles; they were guilty, in his eyes, precisely because they were unfaithful Jews. He would not have persecuted Gentiles, and he could not; he had no authority to do so.

Working with the chief priests in Jerusalem, however, Saul "shut up many of the saints in prison" (Acts 26:10); and "when they were put to death," he said, "I cast my vote against them." He persecuted Christians "violently" (Gal. 1:13)—"to the death, binding and delivering to prison both men and women" (Acts 22:4). His goal was nothing short of the destruction of the Church (Gal. 1:13).

The growth of the Church surely fueled his fury. He believed he was on a divine mission—"as to zeal a persecutor of the church, as to righteousness under the law blameless" (Phil. 3:6).

As he traveled to bring the persecution to Damascus, however, something happened.

What happened was an event of seismic importance to the early Church. The story is told not once, but four times in the New Testament, three times in the Acts of the Apostles alone.[46] Here is the story in Saul's words, as related by St. Luke.

---

[46]The incident on the road to Damascus appears in Acts 9:3–9, 22:6–11, and 26:12–19 and Galatians 1:12–17. A passing reference occurs in 1 Corinthians 15:8.

As I made my journey and drew near to Damascus, about noon a great light from heaven suddenly shone about me. And I fell to the ground and heard a voice saying to me, "Saul, Saul, why do you persecute me?" And I answered, "Who are you, Lord?" And he said to me, "I am Jesus of Nazareth whom you are persecuting." Now those who were with me saw the light but did not hear the voice of the one who was speaking to me. And I said, "What shall I do, Lord?" And the Lord said to me, "Rise, and go into Damascus, and there you will be told all that is appointed for you to do." And when I could not see because of the brightness of that light, I was led by the hand by those who were with me, and came into Damascus. (Acts 22:6–11)

Saul had been correct in his sense of personal destiny. God did indeed have a mission for him—something "appointed" for him to do. He had been right, too, that he was destined to bring about the fulfillment of prophecy. He was wrong, however, about the identity and the day of the Messiah.

As he lay on the ground, he knew that he was facing almighty God, but he recognized also that he did not know God. He addressed the voice as "Lord," but asked him, "Who are you?"

The response he received was curious: "I am Jesus … whom you are persecuting." What could it mean? By that time, Jesus himself had been out of the picture for years. Saul had not been persecuting Jesus, but rather Jesus' followers. Neither Saul nor Luke bothered to explain the phrase as they told the tale. But those few words would come to inform so much of Saul's later doctrine, as he wrote and preached under his

Greek name, Paul. He would speak often of the Church as Christ's Body on earth. To the Corinthians he wrote: "Now you are the body of Christ and individually members of it" (1 Cor. 12:27). Writing to the Ephesians, he repeatedly identified the two, Church and Christ: "the Church ... is his body, the fulness of him who fills all in all (Eph. 1:22–23; see also 4:12 and 5:29–30). He spoke similarly to the Colossians: "Now I rejoice in my sufferings for your sake, and in my flesh I complete what is lacking in Christ's afflictions for the sake of his body, that is, the church" (Col. 1:24).

So close was the communion of Christ with each believer that Paul came to see his former persecutions as blasphemy directed against God—although that had certainly not been his intention: "I formerly blasphemed and persecuted and insulted him; but I received mercy because I had acted ignorantly in unbelief" (1 Tim. 1:13).

Saul underwent a true conversion. He ceased to be a persecutor of Jesus and began to be a disciple. He converted, but he did not abandon the religion of Israel. Long after his incident on the road to Damascus, he made it clear that he was still a Jew (Acts 21:39) and still a Pharisee (Acts 23:6). The people of Israel would always be, for him, "my brethren, my kinsmen by race" (Rom. 9:3). Accepting the Messiah was not something alien to his Jewishness. Indeed, for all the time he was a Pharisee, it is what he had been waiting for, working for—and even persecuting for. He could honestly say that, as both a Pharisee and a Christian, he had "lived before God in all good conscience up to this day" (Acts 23:1).

Preaching as Paul, he was still a man of the Tribe of Benjamin. As he proclaimed the gospel of Jesus, he was trying not to draw Jews away from Judaism but rather to show them that the ancient prophecies had come to fulfillment. In the words of N.T. Wright, Paul's preaching to Jews was a "critique from within," like that of the prophets.

Rabbi Jacob Neusner, a modern biblical scholar, extends that judgment to the entire primitive Church. Like other groups that diverged from the Pharisees and Sadducees, like the Essenes and the followers of Philo of Alexandria:

> The earliest Christians, Jesus and his family and Paul, all saw themselves as "Israel" and called on Scripture to provide the framework of interpretation of the life and teachings, death and resurrection, of Jesus Christ. All of these groups fall into the category "Judaisms," though each differs in fundamental ways from the others.

In later years, centuries, and millennia, Jews and Christians would distance themselves from one another. There would be a parting of the ways—although when (and even if) it happened is subject to much debate and discussion.[47] It did not happen with—or within—the saint formerly known as Saul of Tarsus.

---

[47] The literature on this question is vast. See Daniel Boyarin, *Border Lines: The Partition of Judaeo Christianity* (Philadelphia: Penn, 2004); Adam H. Becker and Annette Yoshiko Reed, eds., *The Ways That Never Parted: Jews and Christians in Late Antiquity and the Early Middle Ages* (Minneapolis, MN: Fortress Press, 2007); Fabian E. Udoh, *Redefining First-Century Jewish and Christian Identities* (Notre Dame, IN: Notre Dame, 2008); Stephen G. Wilson, *Related Strangers: Jews and Christians 70–170 A.D.* (Minneapolis, MN: Fortress Press, 1995); Oskar Skarsaune, *In the Shadow of the Temple: Jewish Influences on Early Christianity* (Downers Grove, IL: InterVarsity Press, 2002).

CHAPTER 8

Communion

Communion is the condition of fellowship among those who share a covenant relationship with one another. In Hebrew the word for this bond is *chaburah*. In Greek it is *koinonia*.

Communion is a kind of friendship, but it is more than that. It is more like a family bond; and both Hebrew and Greek usage, in the time of the Apostles, suggested a religious dimension to the bond. The word *chaburah* described a group of friends who gathered for religious discussion and common prayer. They met weekly on the eve of the Sabbath (and the eve of holy days) for a formal meal. A rabbi held *chaburah* with his disciples. It was customary to serve fish at such a dinner, and the historian of Judaism Erwin Goodenough has proposed this ancient tradition as the distant ancestor of the modern parish fish fry.[48] In the most ancient images of the Last Supper, Jesus and the Apostles are often depicted seated at table around a large platter of fish.[49] They are gathered in *chaburah*, *koinonia*, fellowship, communion.

A *communion* is something more than a *community*. It is closer-knit, gathered for the most important purpose on earth as well as the most festive. It is defined by a common meal and sacred conversation. For the Jews of Jesus' time, such a meal renewed their most basic identity—as Israel, as God's chosen people. According to biblical theologian Scott Hahn, "The divine covenant brought about powerful fellowship among the People of God."

> But the Jews stopped short of describing any *chaburah* between God and any human beings. They believed such communion to be impossible. The very idea would be an affront to God's transcendence.[50]

Although the Jews shared a covenant with God, they dared not go the extra step and call it a communion. Yet, for Christians, God's Incarnation changed the terms of the divine-human relationship. God had made a New Covenant in the blood of Christ, and he had done so at a *chaburah* meal (Luke 22:20). At

---

[48] Erwin Goodenough, *Jewish Symbols in the Greco-Roman Period*, vol. 5: *Fish, Bread, and Wine* (New York: Pantheon, 1956), 44–46.

[49] Mike Aquilina and Lea Marie Ravotti, *Signs and Mysteries: Revealing Ancient Christian Symbols* (Huntington, IN: Our Sunday Visitor, 2008), 24–32.

[50] Scott Hahn, *Signs of Life: 40 Catholic Customs and Their Biblical Roots* (New York: Doubleday, 2009), 39. See also Joseph Cardinal Ratzinger, *Behold the Pierced One: An Approach to a Spiritual Christology* (San Francisco: Ignatius Press, 1986), 83–85.

that meal, Jesus—God incarnate—declared his disciples to be no longer slaves, but friends (John 15:15). He sanctified them through his blood (Heb. 13:12). The shared blood of Jesus made it possible for his disciples to "enter the sanctuary" and enjoy communion with God (Heb. 10:19). Through the Incarnation, Jesus made it possible for his disciples to enjoy a share of his own eternal sonship, by sharing in his flesh and blood (Heb. 2:14). The language of *sharing*, so often used by the Apostles, is the language of communion—the verb form of the noun *koinonia*.

When Jesus consecrated bread and wine and declared it to be his Body and Blood, he commanded his Apostles: "Do this in remembrance of me" (Luke 22:19). Thus he established, for all time, the model and source of communal life for his *chaburah*.

The Acts of the Apostles presents the Church as such a communion: "And they devoted themselves to the apostles' teaching and fellowship [*koinonia*], to the breaking of bread and the prayers" (Acts 2:42).

The "breaking of the bread" was, ever afterward, the sign of the Church's fellowship and of communion with God. St. Paul asked the Corinthians: "The cup of blessing which we bless, is it not a participation [*koinonia*] in the blood of Christ? The bread which we break, is it not a participation [*koinonia*] in the body of Christ?" (1 Cor. 10:16).

Paul went a step further. He said that the bread was the cause and the sign of the Church's unity. Because the bread is Christ's Body—and the children *share* in that Flesh and Blood—the Church is Christ's Body. "Because there is one bread, we who are many are one body, for we all partake of the one bread" (1 Cor. 10:17).

The ritual meal, then—Holy Communion, as we have come to know it—is the most vivid expression of the reality Christ revealed to Paul (Saul) on the road to Damascus. God's people have become God's Body. They have been invited to share God's inner life (2 Pet. 1:4), "called into the fellowship [*koinonian*] of his Son, Jesus Christ our Lord" and of the Holy Spirit (cf. 1 Cor. 1:9; 2 Cor. 13:14).[51]

Their union with God is closer than they had ever known to be possible. And so was the union of Christians with one another.

* * *

Twice at the Last Supper, Jesus gave his disciples an explicit instruction for their life together: "A new commandment I give to you, that you love one another; even as I have loved you, that you also love one another" (John 13:34; 15:12).

St. John elaborates on this principle in his first letter. He begins by speaking of the Incarnation; he repeatedly uses forms of the word *koinonia—communion, fellowship,* which is made possible through the blood of Christ.

That which was from the beginning, which we have heard, which we have seen with our eyes, which we have looked upon and touched with our hands, concerning the word of life—the life was made manifest, and we saw it, and testify to it, and proclaim to you the eternal life which was with the Father and was made manifest to us—that which we have seen and heard we

---

[51] The passage from the second letter of St. Peter also uses a form of *koinonia*, when it describes Christians as "partakers [*koinonoi*] of the divine nature."

proclaim also to you, so that you may have *fellowship* with us; and our *fellowship* is with the Father and with his Son Jesus Christ.... If we say we have *fellowship* with him while we walk in darkness, we lie and do not live according to the truth; but if we walk in the light, as he is in the light, we have *fellowship* with one another, and the blood of Jesus his Son cleanses us from all sin. (1 John 1:1–3, 6–7, emphasis added)

God had drawn his people, collectively, into fellowship with him. They could not sustain that relationship with him unless they kept communion with one another.

As the story of the Apostles moves forward, the circle of that communion grows ever wider. Persecution forces the disciples to leave Jerusalem, and they take the gospel with them—to Samaria, to Antioch, and even to Damascus. Philip the deacon encounters an Ethiopian, an official of the royal court, and leads him to faith in Christ. The Samaritans—Israelites who had for centuries been estranged from Temple worship—are brought into fellowship when they receive the gospel.

Fellowship does not depend on race, ethnicity, or past history. Even the most notorious enemies of Christ are welcome to communion, if they repent. After his conversion, Paul was delighted to share "the right hand of fellowship [*koinonias*]" with the inner circle of Jesus' original disciples: Peter, James, and John (see Gal. 2:9).

* * *

The sign of the Church's deep fellowship was "the breaking of the bread." (Acts 2:42, 46; 20:7; see also Luke 24:35). The disciples of Jesus shared among themselves the common ritual meal their Master had established. As in friendship or family, the meal was a sign of the bond, and the shared meal strengthened the bond.

Anthropologists call this *commensality*—which they define as "table fellowship," the act or practice of eating at the same table.[52] It was an essential element in Old Testament covenants; the Eucharistic meal was the divinely ordained occasion of the New Covenant. Now table fellowship was shared not only between Jews and Gentiles, but also between men and God.

Commensality was an intense concern of St. Paul as he established churches. Table fellowship is a central theme of his four most important letters: Romans, First and Second Corinthians, and Galatians. The Jewish Christians in Rome and Galatia, even after accepting the Way of Jesus, preferred not to share their table with Gentiles. Some Gentile Christians in Corinth thought they could live immoral lives and then present themselves to receive *divine* life in Holy Communion.

The Apostle saw clearly that these transgressions were contrary to Jesus' intention and destructive to the life of the Church.

To the immoral he spoke sobering words, insisting that anyone who "eats the bread or drinks the cup of the Lord in an unworthy manner" is "guilty of profaning the body and blood of the Lord" and "has earned the punishment of death" (1 Cor. 11:27, 29–30).

---

[52] Gillian Feeley-Harnik, *The Lord's Table: The Meaning of Food in Early Judaism and Christianity* (Washington, DC: Smithsonian, 1994), 11–12.

To the Romans he said: "Do not, for the sake of food, destroy the work of God" (Rom. 14:20). In Jewish culture, to refuse to eat together was to sever a relationship (see 1 Sam. 20:34) and even to declare one another as enemies.[53] To refuse hospitality to Gentiles was like sexual immorality in that it was a profanation of the Lord's Body and Blood. For Christ, by his Cross, had "opened a door of faith to the Gentiles" (Acts 14:27) and sent salvation to them (Acts 28:28).

In the Old Testament, the Jews had segregated themselves in order to avoid pollution by the idolatry—the contagious impurity—of the Gentiles. In the New Testament, God has sacramentally endowed his people with "contagious holiness."[54]

* * *

The Apostles immediately observed the rite as Jesus had commanded. "He was known to them in the breaking of the bread" (Luke 24:35). Paul established the rite wherever he went, not as something he was inventing, but as something he had "received" (1 Cor. 11:23)—something that was already well established.

Paul, however, contributed a necessary theological reflection on the Eucharistic mystery. Jesus did not promise the kind of power sought by magicians (see Acts 8:18–24). He promised a power like his own, which was "made perfect in weakness" (2 Cor. 12:9)—even the weakness of repentant sinners and converted Gentiles.

---

[53] See Feeley-Harnik, *The Lord's Table*, 86.

[54] I borrow the terms *contagious impurity* and *contagious holiness* from Craig L. Blomberg, *Contagious Holiness: Jesus' Meals with Sinners* (Downers Grove, IL: InterVarsity, 2005).

Begun in Baptism, Christian life was renewed in the breaking of the bread. Everywhere in his letters, St. Paul recognizes the mingling of lives that marks Christian communion.

> I have been crucified with Christ; it is no longer I who live, but Christ who lives in me; and the life I now live in the flesh I live by faith in the Son of God, who loved me and gave himself for me. (Gal. 2:20)

To live in Christ is to be filled with his Spirit, the spirit of sonship: the Holy Spirit. For that reason—and only for that reason—Christians could call God Father.

> When we cry, "Abba! Father!" it is the Spirit himself bearing witness with our spirit that we are children of God. (Rom. 8:15)

The ordinary sacramental life of the Church had bestowed an extraordinary gift. It was, for the disciples, a profound sharing in the life of the Trinity. Throughout the Apostolic age, we encounter Christians filled with the Holy Spirit, united with Jesus Christ, and calling upon God as their Father. This was a life unprecedented, unimagined, and unknown before Christ founded the Church.

The Church has the power to live in communion because it shares the life of the Blessed Trinity. Christ has made this possible because he assumed human nature—taking on flesh—and then bestowed his Spirit.

> There is one body and one Spirit, just as you were called to the one hope that belongs to your call, one Lord, one faith, one baptism, one God and Father of us all, who is above all and through all and in all. (Eph. 4:4-6)

CHAPTER 9
Rome

And then shall come implacable wrath
on Latin men. Three shall by piteous fate
bring Rome to ruin. And all shall perish,
with their own houses, when from heaven shall flow
a cascade of fire. Ah, wretched me!
When shall that day and when shall judgment come
from the immortal God, the mighty King?[55]

So ran a prophecy set down by a first-century Jew, likely during the reign of Caesar Augustus, while Jesus was still a child. Rome loomed monstrous in the religious imagination of Jews in the Holy Land. The oracle above goes on to visualize flames

[55] Anonymous, *Sibylline Oracles* 3.61–75.

consuming "temples and racetracks, markets and idols of
wood, of gold, of silver and of stone"—all marks of a debased
Gentile culture. Everything would go up with "a stench of
brimstone."

Such fantasies were hardly unique, although other au-
thors, understandably, chose to express their anti-Roman
sentiment in code. More cautious writers identified the
occupying power in ways that insiders would understand—
those who knew the history of the Chosen People. Rome was
equated with Israel's traditional enemies: "Edom," "Babylon,"
or "Sodom." In later rabbinic literature, the most common
title for Rome was simply "the wicked kingdom" or "the
kingdom of evil."

Israel had suffered conquest and subjugation under the
might of many nations, most recently the Greek Seleucid dynasty. But the power of the ancient enemies seemed fleeting,
in retrospect. Rome's power appeared to be indestructible
and permanent, unless God should choose to intervene with
fire from heaven.

Rome was all the more offensive because it imagined itself to be transparently benign and rational. And yet its com-
manding general could stomp heedlessly into the forbidden
inner sanctuary of the Temple. And yet its prefect could allow his troops to carry the insignia of a boar—a swine—into
Jerusalem, a city where graven images were banned and pigs
considered the most vile and unclean of creatures.

Israel had always considered itself a nation set apart. The
Law of Moses, with its strict dietary regime and sexual mores,
enforced a separation from other peoples. The separation pro-
tected Israel from idolatry, which was its constant weakness,
but also from the immoral practices of foreigners: abortion,

infanticide, fornication, adultery, sodomy, homosexuality, and drunkenness. Those who "mingled with the nations … learned to do as they did" (Ps. 106:35). Even the Temple priests, if exposed to Gentile ways, were prone to take up "all the abominations of the nations" (2 Chron. 36:14).

When the people of Israel showed by their actions that they preferred the ways of the Gentiles, God "gave them into the hand of the nations, so that those who hated them ruled over them" (Ps. 106:41). Thus, the Roman occupation was, for the Jews, a judgment, a humiliation that they had earned by their desire to be like other nations.

In some quarters, as we have seen, the anti-Roman reaction was strong—in the school of Shammai, the party of the Zealots, and the apocalyptic visions of the Essenes. When, in A.D. 6, Caesar Augustus decreed a tax census, some Jews resisted to the point of rebellion. Their leader, Judas the Galilean, called the decree blasphemous, because only God could demand a census, and therefore Caesar was putting himself in the place of God.

Others simply prayed that another of Israel's ancient enemies—the Persians, for example—would triumph over the more-hated Romans.

* * *

The Romans, for their part, were offended by the Jews' self-segregation. They derided the Jews' prohibition of pork and shellfish as arbitrary and silly. The Roman historian Tacitus summed up what was probably a common sentiment among Gentiles: "Moses introduced new religious practices, quite opposed to those of all other religions. The Jews regard as profane all that we hold sacred; on the other hand, they permit all that we abhor."[56] In the words of a modern historian: "Jews were considered unsociable, even misanthropic, for the social distinctions created by their dietary laws."[57]

The difference drew the attention of Gentiles of the Greco-Roman world, and for at least a few it became a fascination. Some influential men and women looked into the Jewish writings and recognized their wisdom and moral beauty. They tried, to varying degrees, to undertake the disciplines—although few men were willing to submit to ritual circumcision in adulthood. The Roman philosopher Seneca, a contemporary of Jesus and Paul, complained that Jewish customs had become chic among the nobles of his time. Many, it seems, were keeping a leisurely Sabbath, which Seneca ascribed to laziness, and even lighting Sabbath lamps according to Jewish custom.[58]

Among the Gentiles, some Jewish sympathizers took the further step of attending synagogue services. Called God-fearers, they appear often in the narrative of the Acts of the Apostles, and it seems that they were among the groups more open to the Way of Jesus. Paul encountered them in the Greek cities of Iconium, Philippi, and Thessalonica. In Pisidian Antioch,

---

[56]Tacitus, *Histories* 5.4.1.
[57]John M.G. Barclay, *Jews in the Mediterranean Diaspora: From Alexander to Trajan (323 BCE–117 CE)* (Berkeley, CA: University of California Press, 1996), 436. Another historian adds: "Jews were generally considered in the ancient world to be hostile, prickly people, quick to take offense and unfriendly to aliens," Martin Goodman, *The Ruling Class of Judaea: The Origins of the Jewish Revolt Against Rome AD 66–70* (Cambridge, UK: Cambridge University Press, 1987), 97.
[58]See Barclay, *Jews in the Mediterranean Diaspora*, 307.

it was the God-fearers alone who, hearing the gospel, "were glad and glorified the word of God" (Acts 13:48).

The books of the Old Testament, for all their horror of Gentile ways, foresaw such a day when all the nations would come to adore the God of Israel (see Psalm 86:9; Tob. 14:6–7). The Apostles delighted to see the prophecies' fulfillment.

* * *

There is ample evidence in the New Testament of the Jews' horror of Gentiles in general and Romans in particular. Even Jesus said that an obstinate sinner should be treated "as a Gentile and a tax collector" (Matt. 18:17). The chief priests, for their part, worried that Jesus' popularity would begin to look like another census rebellion—and would bring about a crackdown from the occupying powers: "If we let him go on thus, every one will believe in him, and the Romans will come and destroy both our holy place and our nation" (John 11:48).

Yet the Gospel also sounded a new and hopeful note for the Romans. Both Matthew and Luke relate the story of a Roman centurion who sought healing for his beloved servant. The elders of his town begged Jesus on the centurion's behalf, perhaps assuming that the Master would not listen to a Gentile. "He is worthy to have you do this for him," they said, "for he loves our nation, and he built us our synagogue" (Luke 7:4–5). Eventually, the man pleaded his own case, moving Jesus to exclaim: "Truly, I say to you, not even in Israel have I found such faith" (Matt. 8:10).

The story is significant, because it shows that a Gentile —even a Roman, and even a high-ranking military officer who served under the insignia of the swine—could have the kind of faith that God sought from Israel.

And this story is not unique. It was another centurion who, seeing Jesus crucified, was moved to confess the Master's divinity: "Truly this man was the Son of God!" (Mark 15:39).

Even Pilate is treated more sympathetically in the Gospels than in any other documents from the same time. The historian Josephus portrayed him as an incompetent boor.[59] The philosopher Philo saw him as deliberately and stupidly provocative.[60] Yet, in St. John's account of Jesus' trial, Pilate appears to be looking for a way to release the accused. "I find no crime in him," he said (John 18:38). Jesus himself downplayed Pilate's personal guilt, placing the greater blame on the chief priests who had handed him over (John 19:11).

In the Acts of the Apostles, St. Luke presents a Roman centurion who was also a God-fearer, a man who "gave alms liberally to the people, and prayed constantly to God" (Acts 10:2). Cornelius received an extraordinary revelation from God regarding Peter, whom he sent soldiers to summon from Joppa. By the end of the incident, God had made clear to Peter that Israel's dietary taboos were no longer to be observed, Peter had preached the gospel to Cornelius and his household, and the Gentiles had received the Holy Spirit (Acts 10:45).

These supernatural developments, quite naturally, led to conflict. Jewish Christians of a traditionalist bent opposed what they saw as an abrogation of the ancient law (Acts 11:2–18). They vehemently protested Peter's sitting down to eat with Romans.

The controversy continued as Paul and Barnabas made more converts among the Gentiles. It was settled only when

[59]Josephus, *Jewish War* 2.9.2–4.
[60] Philo, *On The Embassy of Gaius* 38.299–305.

the Apostles met in council (Acts 15) and concluded that they "should not trouble those of the Gentiles who turn to God" (Acts 15:19).

Anti-Roman prejudice was common even in the primitive Church. But Paul's attitude was consistently positive. He had no use for Gentile idolatry or immorality (see 1 Cor. 5:10). But he was proud of his own Roman citizenship (Acts 16:37–38; 22:25–29), and he did not hesitate to invoke Roman custom and law (Acts 25:16). When tried in court, he appealed to Caesar over the authorities in Judea (Acts 25:11).

Luke consistently portrays Roman officials as sympathetic to Paul and protective of him (Acts 25:24–25; 26:31). When Paul's voyage is shipwrecked, a Roman centurion saves his life (Acts 27:43).

The trajectory of Luke's narrative is Romeward. Paul was inexorably drawn there—in spite of many obstacles—"resolved in the Spirit." He considered Macedonia, Achaia, and Jerusalem to be steps along the way: "After I have been there, I must also see Rome" (Acts 19:21). The Lord himself made clear to Paul that the imperial capital should be his destination.

> The following night the Lord stood by him and said, "Take courage, for as you have testified about me at Jerusalem, so you must bear witness also at Rome." (Acts 23:11)

It was God's will. "And so we came to Rome," Luke wrote (Acts 28:14).

It was a day Paul had long awaited. "I am eager to preach the gospel to you also who are in Rome" (Rom. 1:15).

Even though Roman intellectuals were hardly warm to Jews—and even though the emperor Claudius had expelled all Jews from the city a few years before (Acts 18:2)—Rome was where God wanted Paul to be. And so Paul wanted to be in Rome.

We know little about his work there, except that he succeeded to a remarkable degree. When he wrote to the Philippians, he said in passing: "All the saints greet you, especially those of Caesar's household" (Phil. 4:22). He was granted access, apparently, to the echelons of power.

Peter, too, made his way there (1 Pet. 5:13); and Christians would eventually cast the two Apostles as the new founders of the city. The original founders, Romulus and Remus, had established the city in strife, as one murdered the other. The new founders would consecrate the city with their blood, laying down their lives in the persecution of the emperor Nero in A.D. 64. They would be witnesses to the end—martyrs. Their blood would be seed. The Church in Rome would hold a primacy in the universal Church from the first century onward.

All the great names of the early Church made pilgrimage there, to pay homage before the relics of Peter and Paul, and to visit, consult, and plead before the Apostles' successors. Among the apostolic Fathers, Ignatius and Polycarp made the journey. Clement and Hermas lived in the city for a time, as did Justin, Hegesippus, and Hippolytus, Abercius, Irenaeus, and Origen.[61]

"From heaven shall flow a cascade of fire." In a sense, the prophecy quoted at the beginning of this chapter *did* come

---

[61] See Margherita Guarducci, *The Primacy of the Church of Rome: Documents, Reflections, Proofs* (San Francisco: Ignatius Press, 2003), and William R. Farmer and Roch Kereszty, O.Cist., eds., *Peter and Paul in the Church of Rome: The Ecumenical Potential of a Forgotten Perspective* (New York: Paulist Press, 1990).

to fulfillment. Old Rome was indeed brought to an end by fire from heaven. And the fire did make a ruin of the city's temples and idols. But it was not the conflagration the Sybil had imagined.

It was a Pentecostal fire. It was the apostolic Faith.

CHAPTER 10
Christianities?

Icons of the Apostles often show them as almost identical men, with beards of uniform length and undifferentiated expressions—alike as a dozen eggs. There is a reason for that. The artists want to leave viewers with a powerful image of the life of the Church as it is described in the Acts of the Apostles.

> Now the company of those who believed were of one heart and soul, and no one said that any of the things which he possessed was his own, but they had everything in common. (Acts 4:32)

It is possible, though, to overstate the unity of the primitive Church. As much as its members "were of one heart and soul," they were not interchangeable personalities. They were rather, as St. Paul put it, like members of a body. "For just as the body is one and has many members, and all the members of the body, though many, are one body, so it is with Christ" (1 Cor. 12:12).

Jews and Gentiles who followed the Way of the Lord Jesus did not lose their distinct—and sometimes divergent—personalities, interests, emphases, ethnicities, and even spiritualities. The early Church was undoubtedly one; yet it could accommodate men as different in temperament and spirit as St. Paul and St. James.

Paul famously said: "[W]e hold that a man is justified by faith apart from works of law" (Rom. 3:28).

James may have been proposing a corrective when he wrote: "Do you want to be shown, you shallow man, that faith apart from works is barren?... For as the body apart from the spirit is dead, so faith apart from works is dead" (James 2:20, 26).

Christian tradition saw no contradiction in the statements, but rather a lively complementarity. The Church judged both letters—Romans and James—fit to be counted among the divinely inspired Scriptures.

As iconographers have emphasized the early Church's oneness, recent scholars have underscored its diversity. They perceive hard distinctions—and even nasty conflict—between Peter and Paul and between Paul and James. And indeed the Scriptures make it clear that apostolic tempers sometimes flared, and hard words were exchanged between one disciple and another. Paul said that when Peter arrived in Antioch, "I opposed him to his face, because he stood condemned" (Gal. 2:11). Between Paul and Barnabas, too, "there arose a sharp contention, so that they separated from each other" (Acts 15:39).

Some scholars, following after the German historian Walter Bauer, have so emphasized the diversity of the primitive Church that they dismiss its unity as a pious fantasy.[62] They would have us abolish any distinction between orthodoxy and heresy when we consider the documents, movements, and doctrines of earliest Christianity. Some would say that, until the fourth century, there was not Christianity, but *Christianities* —not a Church, but *churches*. They magnify the Apostles' differences so as to mark out separate and equally valid religions.

Yet it is clear, even from the New Testament's table of contents, that the early Church was not scandalized by the tiffs one Apostle had with another. It is just as clear, however, that there were differences—practical, doctrinal, and disciplinary—of an entirely different order. There were differences that could make one disciple angry with another. And there were differences that could separate someone from the Church and from Jesus Christ.

* * *

It did not take long for serious divisions to threaten the unity of the Church. St. Paul lamented the divisions in the Church in Corinth (1 Cor. 11:18)—and he feared that legitimate differences were producing illegitimate factions.

> For it has been reported to me by Chloe's people that there is quarreling among you, my brethren. What I mean is that each of you says, "I belong to Paul," or "I belong to Apollos," or "I belong to Cephas," or "I

---

[62] See Walter Bauer, *Orthodoxy and Heresy in Earliest Christianity* (Philadelphia: Fortress Press, 1979).

belong to Christ." Is Christ divided? Was Paul crucified for you? Or were you baptized in the name of Paul? (1 Cor. 1:11–13)

A partiality for one teacher or another is not, Paul made clear, a reason for dividing the Body of Christ. Indeed, as a body, the Church cannot be divided.

> There is one body and one Spirit, just as you were called to the one hope that belongs to your call, one Lord, one faith, one baptism, one God and Father of us all, who is above all and through all and in all. (Eph. 4:4–6)

Paul considered God's eternal oneness to be the source and model of the unity of Christians. The Church's communion is a share in the eternal bond of the Father, the Son, and the Holy Spirit. Thus, division in the Church is an affront to God. It is a desecration of the divine image.

Still, Paul recognized that disciples were free to separate themselves from the body through immorality or wayward faith. In his first letter to the Corinthians, he directed the Church to cast out a member who was guilty of incest. Such a severe punishment, which came to be called *excommunication*, was intended to be remedial. The guilty party would be confronted with the gravity of sin and its consequences—separation from Christ and the Church—and would change his ways. And in Corinth, at least, it worked. By the time Paul wrote his second letter to that church, the man had repented and been reconciled.

A graver concern for Paul, however, was doctrinal deviation. Paul urged the Romans not to allow themselves to be led astray by false teachers.

> I appeal to you, brethren, to take note of those who create dissensions and difficulties, in opposition to the doctrine which you have been taught; avoid them. For such persons do not serve our Lord Christ, but their own appetites, and by fair and flattering words they deceive the hearts of the simple-minded. (Rom. 16:17–18)

To depart, in any way, from the apostolic teaching about Jesus Christ was to preach or worship a different Christ. It was a form of idolatry, and so it was the most loathsome of sins.

* * *

It is the second letter of St. Peter that gave the Church its enduring term for false doctrine: *heresy*.

> But false prophets also arose among the people, just as there will be false teachers among you, who will secretly bring in destructive heresies, even denying the Master who bought them, bringing upon themselves swift destruction. (2 Pet. 2:1)

Heresies—the word is now a technical term that denotes the denial of revealed truth, the adherence to a religious opinion that contradicts Christian dogma. But in the original Greek *hairesis* was a neutral term meaning simply a personal choice or opinion.

Peter used the word, however, with a qualifying adjective: *destructive*. False doctrine was a choice—the Apostles made clear—that brought "swift destruction" and "condemnation" for those who chose it.

It was perhaps inevitable that false doctrine should come, but it must not be taken up.

In later centuries, the Church would catalog and catego-
rize Christian heresies. Justin Martyr wrote a handbook of
them (now lost) in the second century. Hippolytus of Rome
expanded on it in the third. Epiphanius of Cyprus compiled
his own volume in the fourth century, calling it the *Medicine
Chest*, because he prescribed a spiritual antidote for each poi-
sonous tenet. By the eighth century, when John of Damascus
set himself to the task, there were already hundreds of heresies to be sorted.[63]

Most of those accumulated heresies, however, were varia-
tions on a few basic themes that had already been evident in
the apostolic age. The New Testament books themselves speak
directly to the problem of these "choices" as they emerged.

- *Simony.* The Acts of the Apostles introduces the strange
  figure of Simon of Samaria (Acts 8:9–24). A magician,
  he "amazed the nation" where he lived and made
  great claims for himself. Hearing the gospel, however,
  Simon accepted Christ and was baptized; but, seeing
  the Apostles' evident power, he was filled with envy,
  and offered them money if they would share their
  power with him. Peter cursed Simon for his blasphemous proposal, and Simon was subdued by fear. The

[63]For an interesting analysis of the ancient heresies and their
modern advocates, see Philip Jenkins, *Hidden Gospels: How
the Search for Jesus Lost Its Way* (Oxford, UK: Oxford University
Press), 2001. For an illuminating analysis of one very famous
heretical text, see N.T. Wright, *Judas and the Gospel of Jesus: Have
We Missed the Truth about Christianity?* (Grand Rapids, MI: Baker,
2006). For an accessible overview of ancient and modern heresies, see Richard M. Hogan, *Dissent from the Creed: Heresies Past
and Present* (Huntington, IN: Our Sunday Visitor, 2001).

sin of buying or selling spiritual goods would ever after be known by Simon's name: *simony*. There is some evidence that Simon persisted in false teaching, eventually establishing himself as a foil to St. Peter in Rome.[64] The early Church Fathers called Simon the Father of Heresies, tracing many later errors back to Simon's sin of greed and lust for power.

• *Judaizing*. In his letter to the Galatians, St. Paul refuted the idea that Gentiles must first submit to the entirety of Jewish law before they could be admitted to the Christian Church. Judaizers in Galatia were requiring Gentile converts to undergo circumcision and keep a kosher diet. Paul insisted that these ritual laws had been rendered obsolete by the sacrifice of Jesus Christ. He treated the Galatians' error as a desertion from the grace of Christ "and turning to a different gospel" (Gal. 1:6). The Apostles meeting in council also condemned the practices of the Judaizers (Acts 15). The problem would continue to resurface throughout the early centuries of the Church, but the movements always remained small. The idea of imposing circumcision on adult males offered little in the way of popular appeal.

• *Docetism*. The name was coined later to describe a heresy already evident in the time of the Apostles. It describes those who denied Jesus' true humanity,

---

[64]Stories of Simon in Rome appear very early in the documentary record: in St. Justin Martyr's *First Apology*, chapter 26; in the pseudonymous *Clementine Homilies*; in the apocryphal *Acts of Peter*; and in St. Hippolytus's *Philosophumena*.

teaching instead that he only seemed to be a man. (The Greek word for "to seem" is *dokeo*.) The letters of St. John deal repeatedly with the problem and prescribe excommunication as its solution:

> For many deceivers have gone out into the world, men who will not acknowledge the coming of Jesus Christ in the flesh; such a one is the deceiver and the antichrist.... Anyone who goes ahead and does not abide in the doctrine of Christ does not have God; he who abides in the doctrine has both the Father and the Son. If anyone comes to you and does not bring this doctrine, do not receive him into the house or give him any greeting; for he who greets him shares his wicked work. (2 John 1:7, 9–11; see also 1 John 4:2–3)

• *Gnosticism*. Gnosticism is the name given by later Fathers to the elitist heresies that emphasized esoteric "knowledge" (Greek *gnosis*) over faith and love. St. Paul may have been combating these ideas when he warned the Corinthians: "'Knowledge' puffs up, but love builds up. If any one imagines that he knows something, he does not yet know as he ought to know. But if one loves God, one is known by him" (1 Cor. 8:1–3). Later Gnostics were fond of devising genealogies of pure spirits and gradually distanced themselves from God. Again, Paul may have been dealing with such esoteric distractions when he advised Timothy not to allow Christians "to occupy themselves with myths and endless genealogies which promote speculations rather than the divine training that is in faith" (1 Tim. 1:4; see also Titus 3:9). Gnosticism tended to elevate intellectual pride as a virtue and lead its adherents to neglect charity. Gnostic heresies mutated as they metastasized and endlessly divided. Already in A.D. 170, St. Irenaeus of Lyons was able to write a multivolume encyclopedic work to address the claims of the many Gnostic sects of his day.

- *Nicolaitans.* In the book of Revelation (2:1; 14–16), John, the visionary, reported that he had received two messages regarding a group by this name. The Nicolaitans were active, apparently, in the Churches of Ephesus and Pergamum and were hindering the progress of Christians there. John's oracles are obscure, comparing the group to Balaam and Balak, two false prophets of the Old Testament (see Num. 22). The early Fathers believed that the Nicolaitans were libertines who encouraged Christians to practice immorality to celebrate their liberation from the law. That kind of libertinism may have been a common error in the first-century Church (see 1 Cor. 6:12). The letter of St. Jude also condemns those who "pervert the grace of our God into licentiousness" (Jude 1:4); and, like John in Revelation, Jude compares rebellious Christian teachers to Balaam (Jude 1:11).

* * *

In spite of the efforts of the heretics, the Church preserved its unity, first in the persons of the Apostles and later in their teaching, guarded by their successors.

The Apostles knew only one Church: the "Church of God" (Acts 20:28; 1 Cor. 1:2; 2 Cor. 1:1). The persecutors, too, knew only one Church. Saul had harassed Christians in many places, but he knew that he persecuted only one Church (1 Cor. 15:9; Gal. 1:13). The Roman officials, likewise, showed little interest in prosecuting heretical Christians; Gnosticism posed no serious threat to them. The true Church was one, although diverse, from the moment it was born at the first Christian Pentecost. The Church was universal before it was local or particular. The earliest Christians delighted in applying the term *universal*—which in Greek is *katholikos*—to their Church. "Where the bishop is there is the community, even as where Christ is there is the Catholic Church," said Ignatius of Antioch in A.D. 107.[65] Just a few years later, the story of the martyrdom of Polycarp was addressed to: "The Church of God which sojourns at Smyrna, to the Church of God sojourning in Philomelium, and to all the congregations of the Holy and Catholic Church in every place."[66]

Such was the Church led by Polycarp. Such was the Church into which Polycarp was received by the Apostle John. It was Catholic. To choose anything other than that one, holy Church (so the Apostles themselves made clear) was to make a destructive choice—a heresy.

[65]St. Ignatius of Antioch, *Letter to the Smyrnaeans* 8.
[66]Anonymous, *Martyrdom of Polycarp* 1.

CHAPTER 11

The Next Generation

The Apostles had a healthy sense of human psychology and the dynamics of sin. They were able to foresee the rise of heresies and make provision for the Church to defend itself. They knew, too, the inevitability of death—and the possibility of sudden martyrdom—and so they made provision for their own passing as well. As Christ had called and sent them, so they would call and send others.

This is evident already in the life of St. Paul. Although he received the gospel directly in a revelation from Jesus Christ (Gal. 1:12), he still had to undergo discipleship under the reluctant Ananias (Acts 9:17–19). Later, Paul journeyed to Jerusalem to spend fifteen days with Peter and James; and, after several more years, he made a second trip to the Apostles to confirm his mission. From his elders in the Faith Paul received approval, encouragement—and credentials that he could produce as evidence of his authenticity.

But he received still more than that.

> While they were worshiping the Lord and fasting, the Holy Spirit said, "Set apart for me Barnabas and Saul for the work to which I have called them." Then after fasting and praying they laid their hands on them and sent them off. (Acts 13:2–3)

From the Church of Antioch, Paul received the "laying on of hands"—the ritual commissioning of new ministers by those who preceded them in ministry. It was one of the basic rites of the Church (see Heb. 6:1–2); and it was more than just a ceremony. The imposition of hands conferred what Paul would later call a "gift." Ordained for ministry in this way, Paul and Barnabas could go forth with the certain knowledge that they were "sent out by the Holy Spirit" (Acts 13:4).

The meaning of the act becomes clearer, in Paul's later letters, as he discusses it with Timothy, whom he had ordained.

> Do not neglect the gift you have, which was given you by prophetic utterance when the council of elders laid their hands upon you. (1 Tim. 4:14)

> Do not be hasty in the laying on of hands, nor participate in another man's sins; keep yourself pure. (1 Tim. 5:22)

> Hence I remind you to rekindle the gift of God that is within you through the laying on of my hands. (2 Tim. 1:6)

We know from these few sentences that ordination was a "gift of God," although conferred by one man upon another. We know that it is a supernatural event consummated by the prayers of those who are authorized to give such "prophetic utterance." We know that the gift is given through "elders" in the Faith to those of a new generation in ministry—who will in turn give it to yet another generation.

One generation of disciples proceeded to the position of masters, and in turn they identified those who would succeed them as masters within the Church.

Legitimate succession was always a matter of concern in biblical religion. The book of Genesis is careful to give the lineage of the patriarchs, from the first man, Adam, to Noah (Gen. 5). The book of Exodus takes similar care as it sets down the priestly generations (Exod. 6). The Chronicles make clear that the monarchy was legitimately passed from father to son (1 Chron. 3). Indeed, the Old Testament histories assure us that "all Israel was enrolled by genealogies" (1 Chron. 9:1).

And the biblical concern for lineage did not pass away in the New Testament. To establish Jesus' credentials as Messiah, the Gospels detail his lineage through generations, going back to Abraham (Matt. 1:1–17) and even through Adam to God (Luke 3:23–38).

In the Old Testament, succession took place in the natural order, through genetic transmission. In the apostolic age, we see a new principle at work. St. Paul was a man who made a firm commitment to live a celibate life (see 1 Cor. 7:1, 7–8), and yet he could pass along the grace he had received—by means of the same act by which he himself had received the grace.

The early Church immediately recognized the importance of this gift. Within a few years of Paul's martyrdom, the Church of Corinth, which he had founded, was already torn by disputes over authority. One of Paul's Roman disciples,

Clement, settled the matter with a pastoral letter to the Greek Church. His reflection is deeply biblical and philosophical, but Clement's argument turns on the matter of apostolic succession:

> The apostles received the Gospel for us from the Lord Jesus Christ; Jesus Christ was sent forth from God. So Christ is from God, and the apostles are from Christ. Both therefore came of the will of God in the appointed order. Having received their orders ... they went forth with the good news that the kingdom of God was to come. So preaching everywhere, in country and town, they appointed their first-fruits, when they had proved them by the Spirit, to be bishops and deacons to those who should believe ...

> Our Apostles knew through our Lord Jesus Christ that there would be contention over the office of bishop. That is why, having received complete foreknowledge, they appointed the aforesaid persons, and afterward they gave the offices a permanent character, that if these should fall asleep, other approved men should succeed to their ministry.[67]

As the Father sent the Son, so the Son sent the Apostles—and so the Apostles sent their disciples to serve as bishops.

The bishops functioned, in many ways, as the Apostles had—as ambassadors and agents of Jesus. Remember the maxim we saw in chapter 2: "a man's *shaliah* is as himself."[68] Those who lied to Peter lied to God as well (see Acts 5:4). The Apostles acted in the person of Christ, and they passed that

---

[67]St. Clement of Rome, *To the Corinthians* 42:1–4; 44:1–2.
[68]*Mishnah Berakoth* 5:5.

gift along to their successors. Thus, Clement's Syrian contemporary, Ignatius of Antioch, could tell the Church in Tralles: "you are subject to the bishop as to Jesus Christ."[69]

* * *

As time passed and the Faith spread to new lands, the Church valued apostolic succession all the more. It was a safeguard against heresy. Many Gnostics, for example, claimed to have a secret tradition that was passed down from Jesus himself; since it was secret, it—rather conveniently—could not be verified. Against the claims of the Gnostics and other heretics, the Church could point to a Tradition and succession that were public and sacramental, a succession whose authenticity could be checked in libraries and archives in major capitals throughout the world.

Around A.D. 170, a bishop in Gaul, the land of modern France, wrote:

> It is within the power of all, therefore, in every Church, who may wish to see the truth, to contemplate clearly the tradition of the apostles manifested throughout the whole world; and we are in a position to reckon up those who were by the apostles instituted bishops in the Churches, and [to demonstrate] the succession of these men to our own times.[70]

That bishop, Irenaeus of Lyons, could speak confidently because he himself had an impressive pedigree. He learned

---

[69]St. Ignatius of Antioch, *Letter to the Trallians* 2.
[70]St. Irenaeus of Lyons, *Against the Heresies* 3.3.1.

the Faith in Smyrna from Polycarp, who was a disciple of the Apostle John.[71]

Irenaeus spoke of succession in terms he had learned from St. Paul. It was a "gift" received from "elders," and it was a guarantor of the truth of their teaching. Bishops, after all, were accountable to the heritage they had received and accountable, too, to their fellow bishops. Succession and communion set legitimate authority clearly apart from heresy.

> It is necessary to obey the elders in the Church—those who, as I have shown, hold succession from the apostles; those who, together with the succession of the episcopate, have received the certain gift of truth, according to the good pleasure of the Father. But [it is also necessary] to hold in suspicion any others who depart from the primitive succession and assemble themselves together in any place whatsoever. These are heretics with perverted minds, or schismatics puffed up and self-pleasing, or hypocrites, acting thus for the sake of money and vainglory. [72]

True knowledge, said Irenaeus, was not the sort of secret *gnosis* promised by the heretics.

> True knowledge is the doctrine of the apostles, and the ancient constitution of the Church throughout all the world, and the distinctive manifestation of the body of Christ according to the successions of the bishops.[73]

---

[71] See *Against the Heresies* 3.3.4.
[72] *Against the Heresies* 4.26.2.
[73] Ibid., 4.33.8.

The faith of Irenaeus was hardly a local phenomenon, peculiar to French Catholics. It is evident, in the same century, in the writings of Tertullian[74] in Carthage, North Africa; Clement[75] in Alexandria, Egypt; and Hegesippus,[76] a Jewish convert living in Rome.

At the end of the following century, when the historian Eusebius began to compile the story of the Christian Church, he saw his task simply in terms of succession. The opening line of his *Church History* makes it clear.

> It is my purpose to write an account of the successions of the holy apostles, as well as of the times which have elapsed from the days of our Savior to our own.[77]

To write the history of Christianity, from Jesus to the end of the third century, was to tell the story of succession within the Church.

* * *

This chapter begins with a biblical principle at work in the ministry of the Apostles: the principle of succession and continuity. But our discussion has extended further forward in history than in any other chapter. That, in itself, illustrates the

[74] See Tertullian, *Prescription against Heretics* 32 and *Against Marcion* 4.5.
[75] Clement of Alexandria, *Who Is the Rich Man That Shall Be Saved?* 42.
[76] Hegesippus, *Memoirs*, quoted in Eusebius, *Church History* 4.22.3.
[77] Eusebius, *Church History* 1.1.1. A fascinating discussion of Eusebius's treatment of succession can be found in Vincent Twomey, *Apostolikos Thronos* (Münster Westfalen: Aschendorff, 1982), 21–34.

nature and purpose of the Apostles' action. Their ordination of successors empowered the Church to preserve the Faith in a reliable, verifiable way. The gospel defended by Irenaeus, Tertullian, and Eusebius was the gospel proclaimed by Peter, John, James, and Paul—then passed down from them to Timothy, Titus, Polycarp, Clement, and others.

Long before the closing of the New Testament canon, the succession was well in place. Until the synods of Hippo and Carthage (A.D. 393 and 419), ratified by the bishop of Rome, local churches differed in their acceptance of biblical books. Some rejected the book of Revelation, for example, and the letter to the Hebrews, while others accepted Clement's letter to the Corinthians as biblical and divinely inspired.

It was the local bishop who declared which books were canonical for his territory—that is, which could be read in the liturgy and used for exhortation and discipline in the Church.

As Peter held primacy among the Apostles, so his successor in Rome held primacy among the bishops. The place of honor is observed by all the ancient witnesses. In all but one of his letters, Ignatius of Antioch spoke as a master to his disciples; only in his letter to the Romans did he speak deferentially. He opened his letter by addressing the congregation in Rome as the Church that "presides over love." To him the Church of Rome is "worthy of God, worthy of honor, worthy of the highest happiness, worthy of praise, worthy of obtaining her every desire, worthy of being deemed holy, and which presides over love, is named from Christ, and from the Father." Again, this passage is unparalleled in his correspondence with the Churches in Smyrna, Ephesus, Philadelphia, Tralles, and Magnesia.

Clement of Rome, as we have seen, wrote his first-century letter to admonish a faraway congregation in Greece.

Throughout his letter, he assumed—but never argued for—a singular authority on earth. He said the words of his letter were written "by us through the Holy Spirit."[78] They are words "spoken by [Christ] through us"[79]—that is, through Clement and the Roman Church. It is remarkable that not a single author in the ancient Church accused Clement of arrogance for making such claims. The historians reported his text without comment. The Corinthians themselves—who were the object of his admonition—honored Clement's letter as sacred Scripture, permitting it to be read in their liturgy.[80]

For Irenaeus, earthly primacy belonged to Rome and to the bishop who received its "glorious" succession from Peter and Paul. The Roman Church was, for him,

> the very great, the very ancient, and universally known Church founded and organized at Rome by the two most glorious apostles, Peter and Paul ... It is a matter of necessity that every Church should agree with this Church, on account of its preeminent authority.

Irenaeus then went on to recite the names of the bishops of Rome, beginning with the apostolic generation and continuing through his own time.[81]

---

[78] Clement of Rome, *To the Corinthians* 63.2.

[79] Ibid., 59.1.

[80] See the extracts of the letter of Dionysius of Corinth, preserved in Eusebius, *Church History* 2.26 and 4.23.

[81] *Against the Heresies* 3.3.2. For an exhaustive study of this passage, see Dominic J. Unger, "St. Irenaeus and the Roman Primacy," in *Theological Studies* (September 1952), 359–418. See also Guarducci, *The Primacy of the Church of Rome*.

If he were writing in the Catholic Church today, Irenaeus's letter could stand as he wrote it. He would need only to add the names of 250 popes who have continued the succession from the Apostles.

CHAPTER 12

Last Things

It must have felt like the end of an era. Although the Christian Church was still growing at an astonishing rate, many of the great figures of the apostolic generation were gone. Peter had recently been crucified in Rome, during the emperor Nero's great purge in A.D. 64, and Paul had been beheaded on the same day. James had been martyred in Jerusalem.

Christians continued to gather for worship in the Upper Room—where Jesus had held his Last Supper; where the disciples had met after the Ascension; where the Holy Spirit had first descended at Pentecost. Even as the Jerusalem congregation grew, the Christians kept a great affection for their "Little Church," later called the *cenaculum*, or "dining room."

The gift of prophecy was common during that generation (see Rom. 12:6; 1 Cor. 12:10) as was devotion to the angels (see

Acts 12:11, 15). And during one meeting of the Church, some thirty years after Jesus' Ascension to glory, a leading member of the Church received an oracle from an angel.[82] It was a warning of terrible things to come in Jerusalem. Christians were instructed to leave the city and move to a certain town in the Jordan Valley, a town called Pella.

Surely the incident recalled the words of the Master as he walked through Jerusalem.

> Do you see these great buildings? There will not be left here one stone upon another, that will not be thrown down. (Mark 13:2)

> But when you see Jerusalem surrounded by armies, then know that its desolation has come near. Then let those who are in Judea flee to the mountains, and let those who are inside the city depart, and let not those who are out in the country enter it; for these are days of vengeance, to fulfil all that is written. (Luke 21:20–22)

A terrible day was coming to Israel's holy city.

* * *

That much was evident, even apart from the revelation of an angel. Disaster was looming for Jerusalem. The zealots and other radical groups were growing, and the occupying powers grew increasingly uneasy. As far back as A.D. 39, the Roman emperor Caligula had uncovered a plot to overthrow Roman rule. Furious, he responded by reorganizing the territory and

---

[82]For details of this prophecy and its aftermath, see Eusebius, *Church History* 3.5.3, and St. Epiphanius of Cyprus, *On Weights and Measures* 15.

rewarding the leaders most loyal to Rome. When Jews in Egypt rioted against local authorities, Caligula reacted with the most outrageously offensive order imaginable. He commanded that a statue of himself be raised in the Jerusalem Temple. His aides knew that this would be an act of war, but Caligula—who was known for his violent temper and whom many suspected to be insane—would not back down. Bureaucrats dragged their feet, however, and the project was delayed so long that even Caligula came to see its madness. He reversed his order.

But damage was done. The Jews and the Romans, always suspicious of one another, were now further estranged. Other incidents followed—attacks on Roman citizens became more frequent. Gentiles, for their part, began to taunt their Jewish neighbors. In the year 66, some Greeks sacrificed birds in front of a synagogue, while the Romans looked on and did nothing. Outraged, the Temple priests put a stop to all sacrifices offered for the good of Caesar. The Roman procurator reacted by sending troops to the Temple to make a huge withdrawal of gold from the treasury—a gift for the emperor.

Now came war. From the Roman perspective, it seemed to come from many directions. There were countless cells of disaffected men—and sects of warriors inspired by prophecy. All closed in on the imperial troops and government. So began the bloodshed that came to be known as the first Roman-Jewish War.

The war raged from 66 to 73, but its climax was a seven-month-long siege of Jerusalem in the year 70. The Romans sealed off all the city's supply routes and stopped up its water supply.

Since the rebellion had begun in outlying areas, many people had fled to the city for refuge. Its population was already swollen, and its resources were soon strained. As the weeks wore on, fear mounted inside the city. Jews tried to escape but were captured immediately.

The Roman commander, Titus, had these captives crucified —by the hundreds—in full view of the city walls. The rebels inside could see their kin as they were tortured. They could hear their cries.

Titus hoped that this would inspire fear in the rebels and that they would negotiate a truce. But it had the opposite effect, infuriating them further and sealing their resolve.

Yet the stress of the siege strained the fragile unity the rebels had among themselves. One faction turned upon another. In the midst of one of their squabbles, the city's food supply caught fire, and most of it was lost.

In the hot summer months of the year 70, people turned to cannibalism, according to Josephus. His illustrative story is of a noblewoman driven mad and roasting her own infant son.[83]

By midsummer the Romans had breached the walls, and at the end of July the city was in flames. On July 29, the Temple—Herod's grand reconstruction, which had only recently been completed—was destroyed. Guerilla warfare continued for several years; but the worst had already happened.

The historian Josephus estimated that, by the end of the war, more than a million Jews had been killed and almost a hundred thousand taken in slavery.

* * *

The Christians' removal to Pella, a Gentile town, marked them among many Jews as a people apart. The disciples had made a

---

[83]Josephus, *Jewish War* 6.3.4.

choice to distance themselves from the aspirations of the zealots and other Jewish nationalists. This distance was confirmed,
in the following century, when the Christians refused to take
part in the rebellion of Simon Bar Kosevah (A.D. 132–136). The
influential rabbi Akiva supported Simon and suggested that
he might be the Messiah. Akiva nicknamed Simon Bar Kokhba,
which means Son of the Star, evoking the prophecy:

> [A] star shall come forth out of Jacob,
> and a scepter shall rise out of Israel;
> it shall crush the forehead of Moab,
> and break down all the sons of Sheth.
> Edom shall be dispossessed,
> Seir also, his enemies, shall be dispossessed,
> while Israel does valiantly. (Num. 24:17–18)

The Christians, according to Simon's contemporaries,[84]
would have no part of the rebellion, and they considered the
leader's messianic claims to be blasphemous.

The Romans, for their part, had had enough. They crushed
the rebellion, killing another half million Jews; and the emperor Hadrian commanded that Jerusalem be leveled—no
stone left upon another—and rebuilt as Aelia Capitolina, a
city dedicated to the Roman god Jupiter, whose temple would
be built over the foundation stones of the Jewish sanctuary.
Jews were banished from the land.

Both Christians and Jews saw this action as a fulfillment
of prophecy and God's judgment upon a sinful generation. At
that point, however, their interpretations parted ways.

---

[84]See St. Justin Martyr, *First Apology* 31.5–6.

For the Jews, sacrifice ceased with the utter destruction and profanation of the Temple. For Christians, however, the age of pure sacrifice was just beginning. They recalled that, at Jesus' death, "the curtain of the temple was torn in two, from top to bottom" (Matt. 27:51). The Temple thus had been decommissioned, made obsolete by Jesus' sacrifice.

The Apostles taught in the Temple precincts, but showed little interest in the business of the Temple. Paul went so far as to tell a Gentile congregation: "Do you not know that you are God's temple and that God's Spirit dwells in you? If any one destroys God's temple, God will destroy him. For God's temple is holy, and that temple you are" (1 Cor. 3:16–17). Those words, written around A.D. 55—while the Jerusalem Temple was still standing—would have been deeply offensive to pious Jews, for whom there was only one Temple. To identify "God's temple" with unclean, uncircumcised people was striking, and surely memorable to those who heard and read those words.

It was a recurring theme as Paul addressed one congregation after another:

> For we are the temple of the living God; as God said, "I will live in them and move among them, and I will be their God, and they shall be my people." (2 Cor. 6:16)

> So then you are no longer strangers and sojourners, but you are fellow citizens with the saints and members of the household of God, built upon the foundation of the apostles and prophets, Christ Jesus himself being the cornerstone, in whom the whole structure is joined together and grows into a holy temple in the Lord; in whom you also are built into it for a dwelling place of God in the Spirit. (Eph. 2:19–22)

The Temple now was with the Christians—and within the Christians, whether they gathered in the little Church on Mount Zion in Jerusalem, or in the Gentile town of Pella, or in Corinth, or in Rome. There, in their assemblies, they offered the memorial of Jesus' sacrifice, as he had commanded, the Eucharist. They knew it to be the same sacrifice, which Jesus offered once for all.

The last prophet of the Old Testament canon foresaw the day when this would be.

> For from the rising of the sun to its setting my name is great among the nations, and in every place incense is offered to my name, and a pure offering; for my name is great among the nations, says the LORD of hosts. (Mal. 1:11)

That oracle of the prophet Malachi is among the Old Testament verses most frequently cited by the earliest Christians.[85] It appears, for example, in the *Didache*'s commandment regarding the Church's worship.

---

[85]Malachi 1:11 is cited as a prediction of the Church's Eucharistic sacrifice by Justin Martyr, Irenaeus, Eusebius, Augustine, and John Chrysostom (among others). It appears as well in many of the most ancient liturgies of the Christian East. See detailed discussion in Oskar Skarsaune, *The Proof from Prophecy* (Ledien: Brill, 1987), 439–440; Théophane Chary, *Aggée, Zacharie, Malachie* (Paris: Librairie Lecoffre, 1969), 239–247; James Swetnam, Malachi 1:11: An Interpretation," *Catholic Biblical Quarterly* 31 (1969), 200–209; Carroll Stuhlmueller, C.P., "Jacob's Well," *The Bible Today*, July 1984, 223–225; and Théophane Chary, *Les Prophètes et Le Culte à Partir de L'Exil* (Paris, Desclée, 1955), 184–189.

> But every Lord's day gather yourselves together, and break bread, and give thanksgiving after having confessed your transgressions, that your sacrifice may be pure. But let no one who is at odds with his fellow come together with you, until they be reconciled, that your sacrifice may not be profaned. For this is that which was spoken by the Lord: "In every place and time offer to me a pure sacrifice; for I am a great King, says the Lord, and my name is wonderful among the nations."

Such was the doctrine of the primitive Church. The *Didache* makes clear that pure worship is an offering of bread and wine, with the prayers that echoed the table blessings of the Jews:

> Now concerning the Eucharist, give thanks this way. First, concerning the cup: We thank you, our Father, for the holy vine of David your servant, which you made known to us through Jesus your Servant; to you be the glory for ever.
>
> And concerning the broken bread: We thank you, our Father, for the life and knowledge which you made known to us through Jesus your Servant; to you be the glory for ever. Even as this broken bread was scattered over the hills, and was gathered together and became one, so let your Church be gathered together from the ends of the earth into your kingdom; for yours is the glory and the power through Jesus Christ for ever.

Some scholars consider the ritual portions of the *Didache* to be the oldest Christian texts that have survived, produced no later than A.D. 48—older even than the New Testament

Scriptures.[86] The prayers are Jewish and sacrificial, and yet they speak of sacrifice taking place far from the Jerusalem Temple.

For now the Temple is Christ in heaven, said John the Seer.

> And I saw no temple in the city, for its temple is the Lord God the Almighty and the Lamb. (Rev. 21:22)

And now the Temple is built of believers, who are Christ's body on earth.

> He who conquers, I will make him a pillar in the temple of my God; never shall he go out of it, and I will write on him the name of my God, and the name of the city of my God, the new Jerusalem which comes down from my God out of heaven, and my own new name. (Rev. 3:12)

Now the Temple is Christ. Now the Temple is his Church. So close is their communion.

That is the Gospel of Jesus Christ as it was proclaimed in the apostolic age, by the Church through its ministers and martyrs.

---

[86]On the dating of the *Didache*, see Enrico Mazza, *The Origins of the Eucharistic Prayer* (Collegeville, MN: Pueblo, 1995), 40–41, and Clayton Jefford, *The Apostolic Fathers and the New Testament* (Peabody, MA: Hendrickson, 2006), 20.

About the Author

Mike Aquilina is the author of more than forty books on Catholic history, doctrine, and devotion. *The Fathers of the Church* and *The Mass of the Early Christians* are considered standard textbooks in universities and seminaries. Mike's books have been translated into more than a dozen languages, from Spanish and Hungarian to Polish and Braille. *The Grail Code* has appeared in ten languages since its publication in 2006. Mike has co-authored works with Cardinal Donald Wuerl, theologian Scott Hahn, historian James Papandrea, composer John Michael Talbot, and Rock and Roll Hall of Fame artist Dion.

Mike has cohosted nine series on the Eternal Word Television Network and hosted two documentaries on early Christianity. He is a frequent guest on Catholic radio and appears weekly on Sirius Radio's *Sonrise Morning Show*.

In 2011 Mike was a featured presenter of the U.S. Bishops' Leadership Institute. He wrote the United States Conference of Catholic Bishops' theological reflection for Catechetical Sunday in 2011.

Since 2002 Mike has collaborated closely with the St. Paul Center for Biblical Theology, which he has served as an executive and trustee. He is past editor of *New Covenant: A Magazine of Catholic Spirituality* (1996–2002) and *The Pittsburgh Catholic* newspaper (1993–1996).

He is also a poet and songwriter whose work has been recorded by Grammy Award–winning artists Dion and Paul Simon.

Mike and his wife, Terri, have been married since 1985 and have six children, who are the subject of his book *Love in the Little Things.*

* * *

Books about Early Christianity
by Mike Aquilina

*The Fathers of the Church: An Introduction
to the First Christian Teachers*

The Mass of the Early Christians

*The Witness of Early Christian Women:
Mothers of the Church*

*Roots of the Faith:
From the Church Fathers to You*

*A Year with the Church Fathers:
Patristic Wisdom for Daily Living*

*Signs and Mysteries:
Revealing Ancient Christian Symbols*

The Fathers of the Church Bible

*Faith of Our Fathers: Why the Early Christians
Still Matter and Always Will*

*The Way of the Fathers:
Praying with the Early Christians*

The Mass: The Glory, the Mystery, the Tradition
(with Cardinal Donald Wuerl)

*Living the Mysteries: A Guide for
Unfinished Christians*
(with Scott Hahn)

*The Doubter's Novena: Nine Steps
to Trust with the Apostle Thomas*
(with Christopher Bailey)

*Praying the Psalms with the
Early Christians*
(with Christopher Bailey)

The Holy Land: A Guide for Pilgrims
(with Father David Halaiko)

*Saint Monica and the Power
of Persistent Prayer*
(with Mark W. Sullivan),

*The Ancient Path: Old Lessons from
the Church Fathers for a New Life Today*
(with John Michael Talbot)

An Invitation

Reader, the book that you hold in your hands was published by Sophia Institute Press. Sophia Institute seeks to nurture the spiritual, moral, and cultural life of souls and to spread the Gospel of Christ in conformity with the authentic teachings of the Roman Catholic Church.

Our press fulfills this mission by offering translations, reprints, and new publications that afford readers a rich source of the enduring wisdom of mankind.

We also operate two popular online Catholic resources: CrisisMagazine.com and CatholicExchange.com.

Crisis Magazine provides insightful cultural analysis that arms readers with the arguments necessary for navigating the ideological and theological minefields of the day. *Catholic Exchange* provides world news from a Catholic perspective as well as daily devotionals and articles that will help you to grow in holiness and live a life consistent with the teachings of the Church.

Sophia Institute Press also serves as the publisher for the Thomas More College of Liberal Arts and Holy Spirit College. Both colleges provide university-level education under the guiding light of Catholic teaching. If you know a young person seeking a college that takes seriously the adventure of learning and the quest for truth, please bring these institutions to his attention.

www.SophiaInstitute.com
www.CatholicExchange.com
www.CrisisMagazine.com